GP. 10a

THE KEY TO GOLF

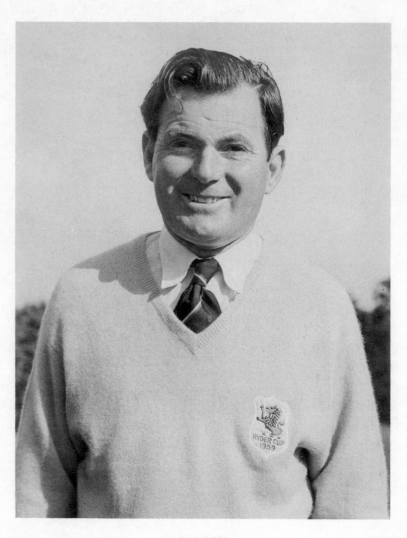

DAI REES

THE KEY TO
GOLF

by

DAI REES

A. S. Barnes and Company
New York

First printing March 1962
Second printing May 1962
Third printing May 1964

Printed in the United States of America

TO MY WIFE

For the past twenty-five years I have had some of the limelight. She has had the task of looking after a house and bringing up a family. Without her help I could not have done what I have done.

All photographs have been specially
taken for this book by
H. W. NEALE
260 Upper Tooting Road
London, S.W.17

CONTENTS

PART ONE

How to Play

THE FIRST STEPS	9
HOW TO HOLD THE CLUB	13
TAKING UP THE STANCE	17
SWINGING INTO GOLF	20
FROM THE TEE	25
THE OTHER WOODEN CLUBS	28
PLAYING THE LONG AND MEDIUM IRONS	31
SHOTS NEAR THE GREEN	35
HOLING OUT	41
GETTING OUT OF BUNKERS	48
RECOVERY SHOTS	52
RECOVERY SHOTS FROM UNEVEN GROUND	57

PART TWO

Common Faults

TOPPING	65
PULLING	68
SHANKING	70
PUSHING	73
HOOKING	75
SLICING	79
SKYING	82
OTHER FAULTS	84

CONTENTS

PART THREE

Odds and Ends

THE MENTAL SIDE   89
BE FAMILIAR WITH THE RULES   93
GOOD MANNERS IN GOLF   97
ON PRACTISING   101
TAKING CARE OF YOUR EQUIPMENT   104

PART FOUR

QUESTION AND ANSWER   107
GLOSSARY OF GOLF TERMS   121

PART ONE — *How to Play*
THE FIRST STEPS

JUST as my last book *Dai Rees on Golf* was written for the very good golfer or the golfer who was on the way to being very good, this book is intended for the golfer who has not yet reached that state of efficiency, although I hope that after reading it that his or her game will improve steadily.

Many of you will have played golf before and will have reached that tantalising stage of knowing (in part at least) what to do but not being able to carry it out. Do not let that feeling worry you, because it is with thousands of golfers all their lives.

No matter how much you might read about the game of golf, no matter how many lessons you may have, in the end the human element has a say. How much you can discipline yourself to do the correct thing every time depends on you and you alone.

There is not a golfer anywhere in the world who does not keep hoping that next time things will be different. It is that hope which keeps every golfer going, and when I say every golfer I mean first-class professionals no less than the merest rabbit.

True, there are people who play golf for exercise and exercise alone, but these people are in the minority and are mostly getting on a bit. For the others the game is a delight and at the same time a continuous challenge. One day the game will be reasonably good—it may stay like that for several games and then things will be as bad as ever.

One of the oldest golfing stories of all, and one which has been related many times, is the one about the old Scottish caddie who was "carrying" for an eminent professor. The learned one was playing a terrible game and asked his caddie for advice. The caddie pondered a moment and after scratching his hair replied, "Well, sir, you maun play wi' your heid," meaning that you couldn't play golf unless you thought about it. That is the trouble with most golfers; they don't apply themselves to the game as they should do.

A great number of people who take up golf achieve a remarkable success at the game in the very earliest days. These are people who have played some other sport. They are natural hitters of a ball and they take to golf like a duck to water—for a time. Then they start to think about the game and soon they are in trouble. Theorising is a very different thing from concentration. In the one you are probing

9

and experimenting, in the other you are applying to yourself well-tried principles.

The game of golf is plagued with theorists who are always trying something new, and very few of them ever get anywhere. They try this and they try that. They listen to everyone who will talk about golf to them. They read all they can on golf and they go on from one professional to another in the hope that they will be told something new which will bring about a revolution in their game. If they only knew it, only they can bring about the revolution and that by perfecting a method of hitting a golf ball well and sticking to that method.

I cannot over-emphasise that point. In this book I am going to lay down the basic principles of playing golf because most people can never succeed at any game without basic principles. But at the risk of being the first writer on golf to say that some people will be able to play golf well without some of these basic principles, I maintain that some can do so, but such people are few.

For instance, there are some good golfers who show more knuckles of the left hand than they ought to. This usually means that the right hand is too much under the shaft. Some people have a pronounced "closed" stance, i.e. their left foot is in front and they look to be aiming away to the right of the target. I could instance many other individual styles which are adopted by golfers and, may I say, adopted successfully. No matter what I say, and no matter what any other golf professional may say, people will always stray from the paths of orthodoxy. I can do nothing for such people except say that if they are getting results and have got results for years then carry on. But I must say this. If you are unorthodox and things go wrong, it will be hard to put them right.

That's why everybody should keep as near to an orthodox style as possible. I think I can watch most of the famous tournament professionals from a distance and identify each one. They may all look alike in their style to most people, but yet they have all developed their own little touches.

I have taught many pupils who have hit the ball reasonably well while still being completely unorthodox. I have suggested to them that they should make one or two changes to bring them back to the straight and narrow, and each and every one has been amazed how much simpler it was to hit the ball in an orthodox manner.

But I am running away with myself. So far I have said nothing about what it costs to start playing golf, and nothing about the equipment which is necessary before you can go out on a course. I feel those of you who have not played before or have played only occasionally and with borrowed clubs would like to know these things.

First-class golfers play on a private course and their equipment consists of a fine leather bag, a full range of fourteen clubs, waterproof clothing and spiked shoes. All that equipment is desirable, but you can do without some of it when you start.

Take the clubs. The local professional will almost certainly be able to fix you up with a set of second-hand clubs or, if you prefer, a short set of new ones. By that I mean five or six or seven clubs. These clubs will be from a full range so that as your enthusiasm grows and your game improves, you will be able to add to them. A bag of some sort is essential, but again it is not necessary to invest in a very expensive one at the start. Most golfers play with spiked shoes, but in the summer at any rate there are those who play with rubber-soled shoes. I advise you to get proper golf shoes as soon as possible after you start to play golf. The same applies to waterproof clothing. You really cannot play golf unless you are correctly shod or unless you are protected from rain.

Although most golfers play at private clubs, thousands play on public courses and many thousands more started playing golf on them. Naturally, if you play only once or twice in a week, playing on a public course is a cheap way to take part in the game. The cost of being a member of a private club varies considerably according to the club and perhaps also the district.

There is much talk of golf being a very expensive game. True, there is the initial expense of buying clubs of some sort and also the expense of joining a golf club if you decide to do that. But please don't forget that once you have bought equipment it will last a long time. There are many golfers who change their clubs often, but that is quite unnecessary. Equipment wears out in time, but replacements are not frequent.

Membership of a golf club has to be paid each year, but all in all the cost of playing golf is not great when you consider the many hours of exercise and fun you get out of it. I have heard the cost likened to a couple of good seats at a cinema once a week.

One of the great things about golf is that you can go to a course and play when you like. You are not tied down to certain hours; and, what is perhaps most important of all, you make many friends whose company you enjoy.

If you are a complete novice it is advisable to have lessons from the professional before you start serious play. I know you may have willing friends who are happy to give you tuition, but learning golf is something like learning to drive a car: it is best to get advice from an acknowledged expert rather than from a well-meaning friend.

Having acquired the rudiments of the game, some people are able to learn a great deal from watching star players. I have to warn you, though, that it is best to try to pinpoint their basic technique. They are highly trained athletes and are very strong. Try to imitate them by all means, but do not be disappointed if you fail to get the same results as they do.

Golf is a very demanding game. You must never be too confident about it, but on the other hand you must not be too timid and nervous. At times you will be depressed at the lack of progress you are making, and you must persevere until things get better. You can take it as certain that no matter how bad you are you always see someone else on the course or the practice ground who is a great deal worse. I have been reliably informed on this point by many pupils, and I believe them. There is no need to be embarrassed at any time. If you are out on a course and things are going pretty badly it will not help if you keep barging on trying to keep out of the way of the people behind. The thing to do is to wave them on and then get down to the business of concentrating on your game. You will find that most good golfers are most tolerant of beginners and long-handicap players.

I know all these stories of peppery retired army officers who are supposed to have apoplexy when held up by bad golfers. Well, these officers are a dying race and anyway they themselves are just about as bad golfers as they can be.

Now I come to what I might call the jack-pot question. And it is addressed mainly to beginners. How long will it take you to become a reasonable golfer? Well, that depends on many things. On how often you can play, how keen you are, how much you are prepared to dedicate yourself to the task of becoming first class.

I seem to remember a great old veteran, Mr. Sydney Fry, telling me a long time ago that he took up golf at the age of twenty-seven and became scratch in less than two years. I should add that Mr. Fry was a fine all-round sportsman before he took up the game—which naturally would be a great help. But that was exceptional, although such a thing is possible. The trouble is that few people nowadays can give up their whole life to playing golf. They have to rely on visits to the golf course mainly at week-ends, with an occasional evening thrown in.

As a rule, improvement at golf is a gradual thing and does not come on in one great leap, so to speak, so don't be discouraged if things go slowly. Usually what happens is that there is one great burst of improvement. And that is followed by a period where the game seems to go back. That cycle is repeated, but nevertheless there is a good overall gain and the handicap starts to come down gradually.

So off we go to the first step.

HOW TO HOLD THE CLUB

THE function of the grip is to hold the golf club in such a manner that it will be fully controlled and will execute the swing properly. That can only be done if each hand transmits an equal amount of force at exactly the right moment. It is necessary, therefore, that the club is held properly. In this respect you will notice I used the word "held" instead of "gripped", because I feel that the word "grip" suggests to some people that they must hold the club so firmly that they are almost frozen.

But to the other extreme, and this is most important, the hands must not be independent of each other. They must work as a pair or a team, and they must allow the wrists to flex as required because the wrists are the hinge on which the whole swing depends.

There are several kinds of grip, and I dare say that the devotees of them all can put up a good reason why their grip is the best. I always listen to such enthusiasts, because after all they have thought things out for themselves and decided that their particular grip is the one for them.

Undoubtedly the most common one is the overlapping or "Vardon" grip. It was made fashionable by the famous professional who was once at the South Herts Club which I now have the honour to serve.

Its popularity lies in the fact that the little finger of the right hand overlaps the forefinger of the left hand, thus linking the hands together. Many golfers like the confidence such a grip gives them, for it keeps the hands as close together as they can be. That is a very good thing, believe you me, because if the hands are loose then you are in trouble from the word "go".

There is a snag with the overlapping grip, and the snag is that it does not suit those golfers with rather short fingers.

If you have been overlapping and have not been getting as much power into your shots as you think you should be getting—this over a long period—then you might do worse than think about the one I use, the two-handed grip.

I've played with this all my golfing life and it feels comfortable to me, consequently it works. Nowadays it is growing in popularity in the United States and several of their best golfers now use it, in addition to many thousands of the rank-and-file. Incidentally, I have my hands very close together and my hands do work in unison.

There is another grip, but not in such wide use now. That is the interlocking grip, in which the little finger of the right hand is interlocking with the forefinger of the left hand. Some long-handicap players use this but I fancy if you are to get results from it you need very long and flexible fingers.

I have suggested that if you are uncomfortable with overlapping, think about using the simple two-handed grip; but on no account change unless you are desperately unhappy and feel there is something very wrong. Too many golfers experiment for the sake of experimenting and it gets them nowhere.

I regret to say there are many golf professionals who want to make everybody play with the overlapping grip and insist that it is a cure for all ills. It is nothing of the sort. The chances are that if you have certain golf faults using a two-handed grip, you will still have them when you use an overlapping grip.

The purpose of the grip is to maintain perfect control of the club from the start of the swing to the finish. If you have that control with your present method stick to it and pay no attention to anybody.

I have said that both hands should be in control of the club. I do not mean by that that you should hold the club as you hold a hammer. I have often likened the golf grip to the hold you have on the steering-wheel of your car: firm, but not vice-like. The hands should always remain flexible and there should be no tenseness at all.

To get the correct grip, put the head of the club on the ground and lay the shaft in your left hand, so that it lies diagonally across the fingers between the centre of your forefinger and the base of the other three. Having done that, you take the shaft of the club with the left forefinger and the thumb. Do not grip tightly but, all the same, grip it firmly. The next move is to close the last three fingers of the left hand over the shaft.

If you look down you will now see that two knuckles of the left hand should be showing. Some teachers insist that you should see three knuckles of the left hand, but I think this is wrong. You will see also that the V formed by the thumb and the forefinger is pointing towards the right shoulder. Do not listen to any club-bar lawyers who tell you that the V should be pointing a good deal to the left. They are quite wrong.

Now add to it the right hand on to the shaft below the left hand, and remember one important point. It is only the fingers of the right hand which go round the shaft. That is where so many people go wrong. I think the most important finger of the right hand, or of either hand if it comes to that, is the forefinger. It should nestle round the shaft, caressing it in much the same way as the forefinger caresses the trigger of a rifle. If you look down you will see that the V formed by the forefinger and thumb of the right hand also points towards the right shoulder.

Overlapping

After that the grips vary slightly, but they should all do the same job of work—transmit the necessary power to swing the club.

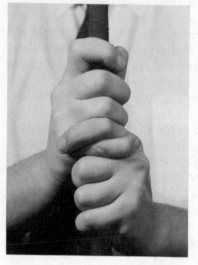
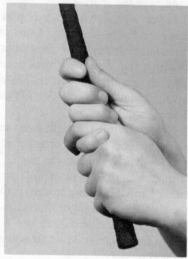

Two-handed

When you check up on your grip from time to time you will find that one or other of the hands has moved out of position. Usually it is the left hand which is the culprit. It often wanders towards the right and the result is a vicious hook. The best thing, even though it is risking the amused looks of your friends, is to check the grip before *every shot*.

If I were asked to say what is the most common fault when gripping or holding a club, I would say it is the reluctance of many golfers to hold the club with the fingers of the right hand. I have told pupils time and again about this, but still they persist in holding the shaft with the palm of the right hand with the result they play many bad shots.

Once you have taken your grip you must not change it or loosen it. It is part of the whole swing system, and a very important part too, for it is when the hands move back at the start of the swing that the other parts of the body start working as well.

The hands are the only parts of the body which are in contact with the club, and consequently their role in the game of golf is tremendous. If more average golfers paid attention to the hands, there would not be so many long faces in the golf club in the early evening.

TAKING UP THE STANCE

I NEED hardly say that the stance is most important. Too many people go up to hit a golf ball without first taking the greatest care to see that the feet are placed where they ought to be placed. This is something I can never understand, for the feet are the only parts of the body which are in contact with the ground, so they must be very important. To play golf you must have perfect balance, and if your feet are not correctly placed you cannot have that balance. I don't care when you go to your golf club, you will see golfers adopt the most unorthodox poses after hitting the ball. They will be leaning forward with knees bent, they will have tied themselves up in a knot, or they will be falling backwards like a man trying to ward off some wild animal.

Why are they doing these abnormal things? Because their stance is bad, so that they lose their balance every time they play a stroke.

Generally speaking, the stance should be square or very slightly open: a straight line drawn from the toe of the right shoe to the toe of the left should be the direction of the intended flight of the ball —this will help you determine whether your feet are square. Or you can do it by laying down a golf club in front of your toes.

The width of the stance should be roughly the same as the width of the shoulders. There are exceptions to this; for instance, a very tall man would need a stance slightly wider than his shoulders, and a small man a narrower one.

Having established the distance between the feet, the next step is to decide how far the ball is to be away from the toes. A good way of fixing this is to place the clubhead behind the ball and drop the shaft. If it touches the left leg just above the knee you are right.

Many golfers, in order to place themselves at the correct distance from the ball, take the club in the left hand and place the clubhead behind the ball with the arm extended but by no means stretched. They then fix the right hand in position and are ready to start swinging the club. The question of distance from the ball is important because many golfers unconsciously get farther and farther back. You should check up regularly.

For a driver, the ball should be in a position just opposite the inside of the left heel. For a No. 2 wood it should be slightly more towards the centre of the stance, but only the matter of an inch or two. For a No. 3 wood another inch or two towards the centre of the stance; and so on with the iron clubs.

As the loft of the irons increases so does the stance narrow, until, for short approaches and shots out of bunkers, the feet are close together and the ball is opposite the right toe.

Some years ago almost everybody played golf with a square stance, but now some professionals are very much against this. They have carefully worked out that if they have the left foot drawn back a good way, or the right foot drawn back a good way, they will be better able to play with a "fade" (the ball finishing slightly to the right of its original line) or with a "draw" (the ball finishing to the left of the line on which it started out).

But what's wrong with hitting it straight? After all, thousands and thousands of golfers would give anything to be able to hit a golf ball straight down the middle yet we have the professionals *trying not to play straight*. I can understand playing with a draw, because by doing that you get a little more distance, but with a fade you get less distance. So what's the sense in it?

I say let these fellows get on with their theories while you stick to more orthodox tactics, and that means a square stance, or a stance very nearly square. I say very nearly square because I myself use a slightly open stance for some clubs as I will describe later. There are

The correct way to stand; the cor- The wrong way. The hands are too
rect way to hold the club on the tee far back and so is the ball

times when you do use a pronounced open stance and times when you use a pronounced closed stance, but these are for special shots.

Having said that I advocate a square stance in general, I must be fair and say that there are golfers who have reached a high standard using a stance which is far from square. They feel at home with it and more than that they get results. There seems no good reason why a change should be made, for I believe to feel comfortable at golf is very important; if you feel comfortable and have the same method of hitting the ball each time then you are well on the way to success, whether your stance is slightly open, slightly closed or square. But things are less likely to go wrong if you use the square stance or a stance which has the left foot drawn back just a little way.

I hope I haven't confused you with all this talk of "square stance" or a stance "very nearly square". What I don't want you to have is a stance which is very open or very closed, because if you do it will lead you into bad habits.

When I take up my stance I have my knees bent a little as if I were settling down on the ground. That is to avoid becoming rigid. After all, your legs play an important part in golf, and the knees must be flexible as the weight is transferred from one leg to the other. If the knees are slightly bent at the very outset, they will be all the better prepared for the part they have to play later on.

SWINGING INTO GOLF

PRESUMABLY even if you are a beginner you have seen golf played, consequently when I talk of the swing you know what I mean. If you have played golf for some time then you will know all about the swing even if you have not yet got it in the correct groove.

What is the purpose of the swing? It is to create sufficient force to hit the ball. You do that through the power you impart to the swing; the greater the power you impart, the faster the clubhead will travel and the farther you will hit the ball.

I am afraid that many golf teachers give the impression that the swing is something built up of different movements. I like to regard the swing as being all in one piece. If you don't understand what

I mean, just try swinging a golf club backwards and forwards. It will not take you long to find out that you can swing it quite far back and quite far forward all in one movement, much the same as the pendulum of a clock moves in one motion.

By transferring the weight to the right foot as the club goes back and transferring it again to the left foot as the clubhead is brought down and using the wrists as a hinge, a good swing can come into being.

I think the wrists are very important in the golf swing. If they were to remain straight as the club is taken back all you would be able to do is to take the club back a short distance; in fact, all you would be able to do is to get it into a horizontal position—a continuation of the arms, so to speak. From that position it would be quite impossible to create anything like sufficient force for you to hit the golf ball hard, so it is very necessary that the wrists act as a hinge and so enable you to get the club to describe a proper arc.

I have mentioned the importance of the wrists. I must also now stress again the importance of the hands. If you are holding the club correctly then your swing will be in one piece and you will feel that it is right from the start; if you do not feel that then I am certain the swing is unlikely to be what is wanted.

Having said that, we then come to the question: What starts the swing, the hands or the hips or the shoulders? There has been almost as much controversy about that one as with the age-old problem: "Which came first, the hen or the egg?"

In my mind there is no doubt at all that everything starts with the hands. It stands to reason it must do, for you haven't the time when you are swinging a golf club to say to yourself: "Now the left knee should be bent", or "The shoulders should turn here", or "Now it is time the hip began to move". It is when golfers start that nonsense that their game goes to pieces.

Anyway, such thinking must go to build up tenseness, and good golf cannot be played when a golfer is tense—sorry to repeat that, but it is so true. If you have a feeling of tenseness before you start the swing, I recommend that you swing the club backwards and forwards a few times until you are perfectly relaxed. If you have a relaxed swing then you will find that the other parts of the body will do their jobs when required; and more than that, if your swing is relaxed you will find that you will be hitting the ball away with a minimum of effort. In fact, you will be surprised at the ease with which you do hit it.

The correct swing: weight transferred to the right foot and the club horizontal

Here the weight has not been transferred. Arms are cramped

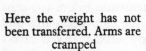

Leaning away from the
ball and swing too flat

It is not necessary to lunge out and bash the ball in order to send it
a long way. Golf professionals don't do that. They hit the ball without
any great apparent effort. Their swing is in a well-defined arc with
the wrists acting as the hinges, so that the clubhead can be taken
upwards towards the top of the swing. You must not flail your arms
out. If you do that then your club will not be in a true arc and the
movements of the various parts of the body will be all wrong.

There is a professional in the south of England, Charles Macey,
who for a time, at least, tried teaching his pupils to the strains of
music. Sounds queer, doesn't it? Yet Macey had something, I feel,
because a sense of rhythm is most necessary in swinging a golf club.
When you achieve that sense of rhythm then you will be well on the
way to playing better golf—much better golf.

I was out with a pupil recently and he had got himself into a
dreadful mess. He started off his swing by bending the left knee in
a most exaggerated fashion. Then having done that he lifted the left
heel as high as he could get it. The result of all that was there was
no arc to his swing at all.

There are many golfers who get by with unorthodox tactics—some of them get good results. But I counsel you not to take up the attitude that golf is an individual game at which you can play any old how. If you have a sound, foolproof swing, then there is less chance of things going wrong and you will be spared what many golfers have to do, doing something else wrong to put things right. Such an expedient can only be temporary.

It really is no good saying to yourself: "Old Smith looks a bit funny, but he hits the ball farther than I do, even if I do all the right things."

If you ever have thoughts along those lines, forget them. Of course, some people get away with murder on a golf course, but that's no reason why you should try to commit murder yourself—that is what you will be doing. Murdering your own game.

Ninety per cent of the good golfers in the world are entirely orthodox, and that should be good enough for you. I am sorry to be so emphatic on this point, but there are far too many golfers going around making all kinds of silly experiments without quite knowing what they are trying to do. I agree that most golfers, except those who are getting on in years, should strive to improve their golf; but experiments are dangerous, and just as frustrating, if not as dangerous, are the efforts of golfers to achieve the impossible.

Many golfers work in offices or in stores or warehouses, so that it is not possible for them to be physically attuned to hitting a golf ball as a professional is. So many people go wrong in this and strain themselves to the limit in trying to emulate the stars. The fact is that these golfers will never generate the clubhead speed that a professional will do. You can only make the clubhead move *as fast as you can make it move*. It will not go any faster than that. But the fastest speed must be the fastest speed that it will move in the prescribed arc. Any forcing will be fatal.

When all is said and done the chief aim in golf is to send the ball straight down the fairway, and I often think that if every average golfer could be sure of doing that, even though he never achieved any enormous hitting, his scores would get lower and lower.

A smooth co-ordinated swing is the key to good golf. When it fails then everything else will go wrong. The question is: How is such a swing to be acquired, and after having acquired it how do I keep it? That is a question worth asking. You can swing smoothly by thinking only of the swing to the exclusion of all other points, like the left heel, the left shoulder, etc. There must never be anything hurried about the swing, and the wrists must always act as the hinge, not only when the club is being taken back but also when the clubhead comes into the hitting area (near the ball). The right arm should never be too far away from the body, although it is a mistake to crush it hard against the right side. This merely restricts your movements.

There is no certain way of retaining your smooth swing. Even the best of players, being human, have their lapses. Usually a faulty swing is caused by the golfer being in too much of a hurry.

The clubhead should be taken back slowly and near the ground at the outset, and the left arm should be quite straight.

Too many high handicap golfers use the left elbow as a hinge instead of the wrists.

Remember what I have said about the pendulum motion. If you can get that going then you have achieved something.

FROM THE TEE

THE object of the driver is to get length from the tee. I need hardly say that the length must be allied to straightness, but that is another story.

If I were asked to say what is the most important thing in hitting the ball from the tee, I think I should say a free, smooth swing. There will never be a good tee-shot when the swing is cramped, yet despite that far too many golfers are hunched up with their arms much too restricted in their movements.

That is perhaps because so many golfers are frightened of the driver. It has got them into trouble on rather more than a few occasions, and for ever after they regard it as an enemy. My friends, that's going the quick way to bad driving.

There must be nothing cramped in the action of taking the driver back. This advice applies to all the woods and long irons, and is something that you should never forget. If your action is cramped you will not have a wide arc with the clubhead. What I would like to see is everybody who is starting golf, and also those who are having trouble with their tee-shots, go on a practice ground for hours and hours just swinging the club. I guarantee that things would be easier for them.

When I talk of the backward swing I must say here that the club-head should be taken back until at the top of the swing the shaft is horizontal. There is plenty of time, so don't rush the clubhead back and have it down like an express train. *Take your time* and you will be surprised how simple the whole operation is.

But I'm going too fast myself. I have already said something about stance. The only thing I have to add to that is that for the driver the ball should be at a point exactly opposite the left heel. People get themselves into fearful trouble because they insist on hitting the ball with a driver when the ball is opposite the right toe. You're trying to be a golfer, not an acrobat. It may be individual, but it is making things very hard.

Few golfers hit a tee-shot without a little waggle of the clubhead. True, many of them waggle because they've seen good players do it. They don't know why it is done. They only know it is done. Well, let me say something about the "waggle".

You cannot hit a golf ball until you feel comfortable, and the placing of the sole of the club behind the ball and lifting it up once or twice does just that. But it does more. It enables you to wind yourself up, so to speak. It is the spring which when the time comes releases the power without which you cannot hit a good shot.

The "waggle" is an essential part of golf, but it must not become an obsession. After you feel completely comfortable then start the stroke by laying the clubhead down behind the ball for the last time and pressing slightly forward with the hands.

But winding up and releasing the spring is only the start of the operation, which above all depends on what is called "timing". Those who have played golf for some time will know what I mean by that, but I will explain it a little so that everybody will be sure of what I am getting at.

You will have realised that the down-swing is all-important in golf, for it is the down-swing and the way in which it is executed which brings the clubhead to the ball at maximum speed.

In the early part of the down-swing the left side is in command because you are hitting against it. If the left side is not braced then your golf stroke will be a poor affair. I am not going into all the things that happen if you are not hitting against the left side. But you can believe me when I say that they are too horrible to think about.

Two photographs of the feet taken during a hit from the tee

Above. As the club is about to hit the ball

Below. As the club has followed through

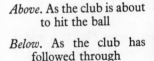

Let us gloss over that and assume that the left side is in command and that the right arm and the right side follow. That being so, it will be the same with the hands. The left hand will be pulling the clubhead down from the top of the swing and the right hand will be always catching up with the left, finally doing so at the precise moment that the club hits the ball. If the right hand catches up too late or too soon, then the timing is wrong and the results will be disastrous.

"Ah, well," I can hear some of you say, "It's all right for Dai Rees to talk about timing—correct timing. But how do we get it?"

First of all you get it by being completely relaxed. If you are not relaxed, then you will swing quicker and things will start to go wrong. I have heard it said that you should have breathed out when your club is at the top of the swing, and that this helps you to relax, but I haven't tried it myself!

Correct timing will not come in a day or a week. It is something you learn by experience, and after you have learned the correct use of the hands which must work together. It is because they so often don't that many golfers do what we call "hit from the top". In other words, the speed of the clubhead is not reaching its maximum just as it is hitting the ball; it has reached its maximum long before that.

The driver is a useful club and it is a dangerous one because from nearly every tee there is a danger lurking. It is your task to avoid that danger, and one way to do it is to tee up the ball fairly high. Many of the drivers made today are very deep-faced and it is best with them to tee the ball up. With clubs which are less deep-faced this is not quite so essential, but if you have a tendency to scuffle the ball along the ground then I say "take a high tee".

THE OTHER WOODEN CLUBS

NOWADAYS first-class golfers carry a driver and a No. 2, 3 and 4 wood. Some even carry a small-headed lofted wood called a No. 5. I don't think, however, you will want to burden yourself with such a battery of wooden clubs, but you certainly need two other woods in addition to your driver.

I have found during my years in the game that many long-handicap golfers are exceedingly fond of playing with a No. 3 wood which used to be called a spoon, and that they are very good with it. I suppose the fact that it has more loft than the No. 2 and is easier to play is the reason for its popularity, and the reason is quite excusable.

But the No. 2 wood, or "brassie" to give it its old name, is a very useful club indeed if your drive has been short and the hole is long. But remember the ball must be lying well. It is surprising how often I see modest golfers put on a show of bravado and take a No. 2 wood from the rough. The result is usually disastrous.

The swing for the No. 2 wood is the same as for the driver. So many golfers make a mistake about this. They think that while for the driver the swing should be a full one the other woods require something that is restricted. How wrong that is. I say again *the swing is the same.*

The stance is slightly different. I stand a little in front of the ball and have my left foot drawn back a little, but you can stand square if you choose or if it feels more comfortable. I use these variations because to me at any rate they ensure that the clubhead reaches the right spot on the ball to propel it hard and straight, but as I have said, you may find the square stance more comfortable.

If the swing is cramped you will hit the ground in front of the ball, and if the swing is jerky and not all in one piece the chances are that the ball will be topped.

I have mentioned that the No. 2 wood is for long shots and should only be played off a good, and I think a soft, lie. The No. 3 wood, having a little more loft, can be played off lies which are not quite so good, and of course if you are nearer the green and think that if you hit a No. 2 well you would go over. For myself I don't see so very many shots from medium- or long-handicap golfers which tear over the green, whether with a No. 2 wood or with any other wood. For myself I would like to see more courage in this direction.

As with the driver—indeed as with all clubs—the swing should be leisurely. If you hurry your swing you can say good-bye to that long shot landing on the green and running up to come to a stop close by the flag.

I shall be mentioning the word "practice" several times in this book, and I say it here and now. Practice is most necessary if you are to improve your game. It is no good going to the golf club every week-end and dashing right on the first tee to play a round. You must practise, and some of the clubs to practise are the woods.

I often watch golfers practising and nearly always I see them sticking to the short irons. I am not complaining about that really, because it is very necessary to save strokes as you get near the green. All the same, it should not be forgotten that a long wood shot can turn disaster into victory and so prove of enormous value to the morale.

When you are playing the woods, several faults can make themselves apparent. There is hooking, fluffing, topping and slicing. I shall be dealing with these faults later, but I will say a word or two about the one I consider the most common—slicing.

This is caused by throwing the arms out so that the clubhead is brought down on an outside to inside arc, thus coming across the ball. I suppose the fact that you are going for distance to some extent makes you throw the arms all the more.

Take your time on the stroke. That is most important. On no account hurry it. This can be done so easily and I think happens most frequently with the No. 2 wood because many golfers have little confidence in it. I find it hard to give the reason, except that as the club has very little loft it appears a difficult club to play.

The result of this lack of confidence is that many people do what we professionals call "quit". In other words, they don't complete the swing; they snatch at the ball and the result is a bad stroke.

With the woods you must go right down and through the ball. You cannot jab at it. If only those golfers who are starting the game and those of modest handicaps would take time, what a joy to them their game would be. I've said that hundreds of times and other professionals have also tried to preach the gospel of leisured swinging, but it seems that it's no good. Golfers go on their own sweet way—which after reflection is perhaps just as well, for if they all did as I say they should, many of my fellow golf professionals would not eat so well!

The secret of good wood play is the wide arc of the clubhead. I must emphasise this because it is so important. And conversely the worst fault in playing a wood is to hurry the shot.

Thousands of words can be written about how to play golf, and many thousands more can be said on the same subject, but when all is said and done the last word is with the individual. If he persists in doing all the wrong things then nothing in the world will make him a good golfer. I can talk about rhythm, uncocking or cocking of the wrists, late hitting and so on, but unless the golfer gets down to business he will not even begin to understand what these mean and consequently he will continue to be in the wilderness to say nothing of nearly driving himself to distraction.

I say all this in this chapter because it is essential to have confidence in playing the wooden clubs and to know how to play them correctly. I know you hear everyone saying: "It doesn't matter for the woods, a twelve-inch putt counts the same."

Maybe so, but there is this to it. If your woods are consistently bad you will sooner or later become demoralised and the demoralisation will go right through your game and you won't even be able to hole that twelve-inch putt.

PLAYING THE LONG AND MEDIUM IRONS

"WHY don't I take turf like a professional when I hit my iron shots?"

That's a question I am often asked, and it is a question that many golfers are always asking themselves.

The answer is a simple one, and it is that golfers who don't take a divot when they play their irons are not hitting the ball when the clubhead is still moving downwards. Somehow or other the idea persists that when the ball is hit with a downward stroke the ball will not rise in the air but will scuttle along the ground. How wrong that is. Let me tell you that if the ball is swept away, or perhaps I should say is hit when the clubhead has started to go up, there is quite a chance that the ball will be topped. Then it *will* scuttle along the ground.

While on this subject of taking a divot, few golfers have ever thought of finding out just where the divot comes from. They know it comes from somewhere and many think that it comes from a spot in front of the ball. Of course it comes from under the ball, which clearly shows that the clubhead hits the ball first and then the ground. I'm talking about properly hit iron shots, of course. The question now arises: Why is it that the average golfer is so prone to hit the ball with an ascending blow? Again I can give a quick answer. It is because the hands are not being used correctly. After the club has been taken back, the hands should then pull the clubhead down. I repeat—*pull the clubhead down*. That means that the hands should always be in front of the clubhead, and they will be if the weight is transferred back to the left foot for that will mean you will be hitting against a braced left side.

All that may seem complicated, but it isn't really. You should think the matter over carefully for yourself and then go out and practise it. There must never be any sloppiness in any golf swing, and there won't be if you pull the hands down, at the last minute uncocking or unbending the wrists so that the clubhead is made to come into the hitting area, i.e. about a foot in front of the ball at the fastest possible speed.

This chapter deals with the long and medium irons—from the No. 2 to the No. 6. The most important difference in playing the various irons is the stance. For the No. 2 the ball should be about the same as it is for the woods, and the process of standing more in front of the ball, or (if you prefer) having the ball farther back from the left foot, goes on until when you are playing the pitching irons when the ball is all but opposite the right toe.

There are changes in the width of the stance, too, for as the number of the club increases so does the stance become narrower—not much narrower each time—just a little. You will soon discover by experience just how wide the stance should be for each club. I am not going to make any hard-and-fast rule about the width of the stance because, as I mentioned in my stance chapter, each individual is of different build, and the width of stance that would suit a very tall, slim man would not suit a short, tubby man.

The stance for the irons should be slightly open with the left foot drawn back. I think that with a slightly open stance you will be able to play a much crisper shot, and there will not be nearly as much danger of heaving the club round your shoulders, an action that is sure to cause a vicious hook.

Many players have the idea that by crouching over the ball they get more power. The correct way to stand is fairly upright. Which means that, as the irons are shorter in the shaft, you must be a little nearer the ball than you are with the woods.

There are variations in swing between the irons, though the variations are small. For instance, with the No. 2 and 3 irons the club is taken back much in the same manner as are the woods, because the feet are closer together for the medium irons than they are for the long irons. With the medium irons the clubhead naturally starts to go more upright. The slightly narrower stance does that, so does the shorter shafts.

"The straight left arm" has been a golf expression as long as the game has been played, I suppose, or at least for a half-century or more, and it remains a very good piece of advice. On the other hand, the right arm is kept reasonably close to the side—not, however, pressed into the side as some golf teachers would have you believe. I do not agree with those who preach that theory and have said and written so before many times. The left arm should still be straight at the top of the backswing, and by this time with the transference of the weight from the left foot to the right the shoulders will be half turned.

For the long irons the swing should be longer than for the medium irons, but I would not worry too much about that because here again this is controlled by the width of the stance. For the long irons, too, the weight should be fully transferred to the right foot during the backswing, but for the medium irons all the weight is not fully transferred and the heel of the left foot should be only slightly off the ground. At the same position with the long irons the left heel should be well off the ground.

The left arm is being straightened to enable the wrists to bring the head of the club down to the ball at lightning speed

I have mentioned the hitting area and talked about the clubhead striking the ball then taking a divot. But the swing doesn't finish there. The swing must be continued and the hands should still be in control with the shoulders having made a full turn since the top of the backswing. The weight should be firmly on the left foot.

Many average club golfers have a fear of playing some of their irons, chiefly the long irons. There is no reason for that fear because it is merely lack of confidence plus the fact that perhaps the irons are too heavy.

Please don't buy golf clubs in a haphazard fashion. Go and consult your professional. He will be pleased to help you. Golfers left to themselves almost invariably buy the clubs because they have a famous golfer's name on them. By all means have autographed sets of clubs—the more you buy the better; we golf professionals like it; but be sure you don't buy clubs which are too heavy. With the latest shafts I find that you can get good results with light clubs, and for those whose hands are not strong like a professional's they are just the thing.

You cannot be a good golfer if you are not a good iron-player, and there is nothing more satisfying than a well-hit iron shot which sends the ball away like a bullet. I say again, the key to good iron-play is the smooth working of the hands. They must be pulled down from the top of the backswing, the wrists must not be uncocked or straightened until the last possible moment, and you must hit against a braced left side.

One tip when playing irons is to take a club big enough to do the job required. There is a tendency on the part of many average golfers to spare the shot, and the result is that the ball falls very short of its intended target, usually into trouble if the shot has been one to the green.

"Never send a boy to do a man's work," they used to say in Wales. The same applies when you are playing your irons; never use a small club when the shot demands a bigger one!

But please don't be scared to play those long irons; if you practise and learn to play them properly you will be well rewarded.

SHOTS NEAR THE GREEN—
THE CHIP—THE WEDGE

NOBODY will deny that this is an important part of the game of golf. Some might go as far as to say it is the most important part, and I don't think I should disagree with them at that.

It is strange, however, that most average golfers are inclined to discount the value of the short game and insist on placing all the emphasis on the long game. The long game is very important, but all the same if you can save a shot near the green you can rectify some of the damage you might have done earlier from the tee or as a result of a bad second shot.

The first step in playing a short stroke to the green is to sum up the situation and decide just what kind of a stroke is required and what club you are going to use; for there are several courses open to you, and the only person who can say which course is to be followed is yourself.

How is the ball lying, is the first question. If it is in a hole or in rough then obviously you will have to use a deep-faced club. If it is on a bare patch then you might decide the only thing you can do is to play a straight-faced club.

In considering the correct club to use you must also take into consideration the terrain between your ball and the flag. Are there any bunkers? Is the ground undulating or is it perfectly flat? All these factors should be observed and taken into consideration. I should say, perhaps, that at the moment it is the fashion to play the wedge for every conceivable shot to the green, but I advise you to use it sparingly. Anyhow I shall have something to say about the wedge later on.

We shall start with the longer shots to the green, and I suggest that the clubs to be used for such shots are the 8 or 9 iron, and always take the club which has a little to spare. In other words, don't try to force a 9 iron when an easy shot with an 8 iron would do. Many golfers overswing with approach shots, especially women. I think a shorter swing, certainly no longer than three-quarters, is the thing. It is compact and there is more chance of getting accuracy because of the greater control.

I think we have already decided that from the driver down through the entire range of clubs the stance gets a shade narrower as you

The correct way to play a shot near the green. The club has been through quite straight

bring each club into action so that for the ones I am now dealing with the stance is narrow. This in turn means that the arc of the swing is more upright. For the very high-numbered clubs, the 8 and 9 irons, the arc is quite upright, thus enabling you to hit right down on the ball with the club striking the ball and then cutting its way into the ground, making the divot fly. Having hit downwards the hands should be kept going right through.

Although golf is a two-handed game, many average players do not

Here the wrists have been turned over and the club is being
pulled round the body. This is bad

appear to look upon it as such when they are playing these little shots.
They seem to get more of their right hand into the shot than they
should, with the result that they flick at the ball, usually just skinning
the ground and fluffing the shot completely. Guard against this;
although perhaps I shouldn't really say it, I think that for moderate
players at least a slightly tighter grip with the left hand is not a bad
thing. At least it does ensure that you do not fluff the shot, which is
by far the most common fault in playing shots to the green.

37

Some may disagree with that, but I think that many bad shots attributed to "head up" are really caused by a weak left hand. I suggest also that you have a slightly open stance and that you should be bold in your shots. Better to be well up than to be short.

So much for pitches to the green. Now we come to the next kind of shot—the chip. This shot should be used when you are quite close to the green and where there are no great obstacles between your ball and the flag. The object of this shot is to make the ball fly over any little undulations but not to go too high. After all, there is no reason to play a high-flying shot when one near the ground will do quite as well.

The feet should be quite close together and a short backswing used. The aim of a chip shot is for the ball to land just on the edge of the green and then run on toward the flag. A number of different clubs can be used for the chip shot. I should say a No. 7 is as good as any, but sometimes I employ a No. 6 and once in a while a No. 5.

Not so very long ago an amateur friend of mine who had suffered for years from being short with his chip shots suddenly became adept at them and being of an inquisitive turn of mind I asked him what had happened. He replied: "Dai, hitherto I used to aim at the pin; now I aim at a spot some four yards past it. Since I've tried that method I am rarely short."

Well, it works with my friend and if you suffer from being timid with your chip shots then you might do worse than try the "four yards past the pin" method.

Have you heard the expression "the Texas Wedge"? It's one Americans use a lot and when they do use it they are not talking of a species of wedge shot. They are talking about using a putter from off the green. Some of the moderns scorn this shot. They laugh and joke about it, but it is a very useful shot. There's no doubt about that and many golfers become very proficient at it.

If the ground between your ball and the green is flat and the grass is short then you can use your putter with safety; but you must always remember when you are lining up the shot that the slightly longer grass off the green will impede the ball to some extent, therefore you have to hit the ball just a trifle harder than you would if your ball was the same distance from the flag but on the putting surface.

It can also be used if the ball is lying on a very bare patch. If you were to use a lofted club from that lie you might play a bad shot, but even at the worst with your putter you should get well on the green and a reasonable distance from the hole.

Then there is the day when the wind is blowing. A high shot, even if only a little one, can easily be affected by a strong wind; but if you play the ball along the ground there is no danger of that.

I'm not sure whether I should have mentioned this when I was talking of little chip shots but a good many crafty golfers, instead of using a deep-faced club or a putter from off the green, use a No. 3 or a No. 4 iron. The reason they take either of those clubs is that they feel the tiny bit of loft in them will get the ball over the longer grass and on the putting surface with no risk of any deflection no matter how small.

Personally I stick to the "Texas Wedge".

Now to the wedge itself, although I am going backwards a little, for the wedge is used even if you are some distance from the green —professionals use them quite a long way off, but I would not recommend that for everyone—about sixty yards is long enough— and if you have no wedge in your bag you need not worry.

The wedge is a comparatively new innovation in the golfing armoury. Now I see that the Americans are thinking up some other ideas—there have been whispers that there is a motion afoot in the United States to increase the number of golf clubs from fourteen to sixteen.

Frankly many golfers are frightened of the wedge, which was introduced originally for the purpose of giving backspin to the ball; but many people have had trying experiences with it because they have not been hitting down on the ball.

The wedge might be said to be a lighter edition of the sandblaster, but with a flanged sole. This is for cutting into the turf easily, but as I have said if you are unable to take a divot anyway, the whole purpose of the club is lost. I have always maintained that any golfer who purchases a wedge should have a lesson from his club professional before it gets him into trouble.

Played properly, the wedge is an attractive and at times a telling shot, but I would advise you to be proficient with the other clubs before trying your hand at it.

Having given that solemn warning I will now go on to give you some hints on playing a wedge because I expect a good many of you already have one in your bag. First the stance. It should be quite open, and if you have forgotten what that is, it means having the left foot drawn back. The knees should be bent a little because when playing a wedge as for other shots you must be very relaxed. In fact, I think that no success can be attained with the wedge unless you are completely relaxed. Some golfers really get down to the wedge. They bend their knees more than for any other short club because they say it gives maximum control and as the ball is not going any great distance a crouch and a restricted arc is the thing.

When playing the wedge take it back smoothly. There should not be any pronounced cocking or bending of the wrists. That tends to make you snatch at the ball. As to the distance the club should be taken back I say that if the clubhead comes up to the right shoulder you are about right. That is the maximum. If you are quite near the green and the main object is to clear some hazard which is in front of your nose then an even shorter swing will do.

You must hit the ball a descending blow. I must emphasise that again, and there is one other point to remember about playing a wedge. That is there is a minimum of foot movement. The putter apart, there is less foot movement with the wedge than with any other club.

I know I keep harping on this downward hitting, and I can hear some of you asking the question: "That's all right, but if I haven't got the strength in my hands, how can I hit a strong downward blow?"

The only answer I can think of to that one is that you must strengthen your hands, and if you are keen enough then you can do that by getting hold of a couple of those rubber balls that some dog-owners keep for their pets. Squeeze them for odd periods of the day and gradually you will find your hands will be stronger.

That advice is given to those who work in offices and such-like establishments. Those who use their hands in their work will not need any advice from me about strengthening their hands!

For any shots near the green, the wedge and others, take your time. None of them should be hurried. Keep your head well down over the ball. This is practical advice, I fancy, because you may have played several bad shots on the hole before you have reached the position of being near the green, and being human you may be rather hot under the collar. Some people, when they are tempted to use a word they ought not to use, count ten. Something of the kind is indicated when things have been going badly and some astronomical score is looming up.

The thing is to say to yourself: "I must get this ball at the side of the hole, so I must be calm about the whole operation." You must shut your mind to the bad shots which have gone before and concentrate on the shot on hand. That is the only frame of mind in which to play a wedge or any other little shot around the green.

HOLING OUT

WELL, we had to come to the subject of putting sooner or later. It is strange that in every round of golf, even rounds played by the best players, some thirty shots are expended on the greens. Just fancy, almost a half of the strokes on a full-length golf course of some six thousand yards are hit on the eighteen greens which each measure no more than twenty yards from back to front.

Mistakes on the greens are not confined to moderate golfers. Even the greatest take three putts on occasion and I have heard of four and even five putts. I must say at once that while the aim should be to get down in one putt the general aim should be to get so close to the hole with your first putt that you are all but certain to get down in two. True, much depends on how close to the flagstick you put your approach shots, but even "rabbits" do get their approaches near the flag on occasion. I think that for a moderate handicap man thirty-six putts on a round will just about do, but many average players, particularly those who have played golf for a long time and have got a little shorter with the years, have become most proficient at putting and make up for their lack of length by good work on the greens.

As a rule these men have had one system of putting all their golfing lives, and what is more most of them have retained the same putter. It is perhaps very human that after a spell of bad putting a golfer should throw the culprit into the lumber-room and gain possession of some new implement which at the outset promises to work miracles. The miracles may come for a time, but after a spell the bad old habits start all over again.

You see, it is not the putter that is at fault when you miss putts. It might be that a putter is too heavy or too light for you, that it might have a little loft on the face when one which is straight-faced is more suitable, but generally speaking it is not the club but the golfer at the end of the shaft who is to blame.

Nerves come into putting perhaps more than into any other department of the game, and it is nerves—or as we professionals say "yips" —which cause the trouble. I have known of famous professionals who reached such a state of nerves on putting greens that they simply could not get the putter off the ground, never mind strike the ball towards the hole.

Admittedly professionals have much at stake when they are putting, a missed putt might cost a championship and the eventual loss of thousands of pounds. For the ordinary club man there is not so much at stake, but even then nerves do play an important part in putting.

It is obvious that to be relaxed is of the utmost importance. Without being relaxed there can be no confidence and with no confidence there can be no good results on the green.

The first thing to instil confidence is to have a good look at where the ball is lying in relation to the hole, to examine the slope of the green if any, the dryness or wetness of the grass and whether the green is even or rough. This is called "reading the green". That is what professionals are doing when they walk round the green, look at the hole from behind the ball, look at the ball from behind the hole and generally take stock of the situation.

They are not "playing to the gallery" as some ill-informed spectators think. Everything they do is done with a purpose, and while I know that the average club golfer does not feel like taking so much time over a putt nevertheless everybody—and when I say that, I mean everybody—must take stock of the situation, otherwise he will be sadly out of touch, and if the ball does finish anywhere near the hole it will be more by luck than good guidance.

How far is your ball from the hole and how hard will you have to hit it? You should be able to judge the distance from standing by the ball and looking at the hole. From that position, too, you will also be able to see whether there is any slope on the green. If the ground slopes down from right to left then you have to make allowance for that by striking the ball to the right of the hole. The reverse is the case if the slope is from left to right. Is the putt a downhill one or an uphill one or is the ground completely level? You must make a decision about that. If uphill you will have to hit the ball harder, if downhill you will have to hit it more gently.

The same technique applies according to whether the grass is wet and lush or dry and fast. In such cases I always aim at a spot about a foot behind the hole if the grass is wet, and at a spot some inches short of the hole if the green is very fast—now I am talking of putts of a reasonable length.

You have seen me, and perhaps more particularly the great South African, Bobby Locke, going up and peering at the hole or seemingly peering at the hole. We are not doing that in the hope that a snake will jump out. What we are doing is having a good look at the grass around the hole. We want to know whether the ground is just a little downhill there and to see what the texture of the grass is like, for the side of the hole is where the grass can be bristly or can be worn.

You might well think to yourself, "Well that's all right for Dai Rees and these people, but is it all that important to fellows who play off eighteen handicap?" The answer to that is, if you don't worry much about your putting you will always be eighteen handicap.

So much for what we call "reading the greens"; now for the actual action of trying to get the ball into the hole.

Having decided that the putt is a straight one or that you will have to aim to the right or left of the hole, then I say stick to your decision. Many, many putts are missed by players who change their mind at the last minute, many of these changes being brought about by nerves. You stick to your original decision and scorn all last-minute changes.

Any day at your golf club you will see many different styles of putting, and some of the most unorthodox will be the most effective. This proves nothing at all except that putting is the most individual department of golf and will always remain so despite those people who are always discovering some new system which is going to revolutionise putting.

Some years ago stroking the ball into the hole was the thing—nothing else was any good; and just recently, all because some Americans tap the ball instead of stroking it, tapping the ball has become the fashion. Then there are those who use a centre-shafted putter as a croquet mallet. Reports of these enthusiasts indicate that this method is most successful until you see the players in action when there is a little pressure on. Then it fails miserably.

Of course the great thing in putting is to be completely comfortable, but if you can be comfortable and at the same time be orthodox then you are on the right lines.

TAKING BACK THE PUTTER

The right way

The wrong way

The next essential, no matter what kind of style you use, is to have your head right over the ball. Some people putt, and putt well on the left foot, and some of the older players do the opposite, they put the

HITTING THE PUTT

The right way

The wrong way

weight on the right foot, using at the same time a very open stance. In such cases the head is not over the ball, but such styles can be dangerous.

Up till now we have mentioned tapping the ball into the hole and stroking the ball into the hole. We have also mentioned that the weight can be either on the left foot or on the right foot. The question now is to sort out what is the soundest method for the great majority. I have no hesitation in saying that the answer is to use a combination of tapping the ball and stroking it and to *have the weight equally distributed on either foot.*

Going on from there let us take the grip first. I myself use what is called the reverse overlapping grip, i.e. the index finger of the left hand overlaps the last two fingers of the right hand. Many golfers use this grip because they feel that it gives them extra steadiness.

I suppose that of all grips for putting the ordinary overlapping grip is the most popular. In other words, most people use that grip for putting because most people use that grip when playing other golf shots. The message would seem to be that the ordinary golf grip should be good enough for putting.

There are quite a number of golfers who use an ordinary grip, but who have the forefinger of the right hand down behind the shaft. Someone, I think it was Gene Sarazen, called this "the after-forty grip"; but it's not a bad idea for those golfers who are still a long way from that age.

Now the feet. I think they should be close together and firmly set on the ground. There must be no wavering about, for that will be enough to get your position off the line. They should be at a right angle to the intended line of the ball.

Using a combination of tapping and stroking the ball you take the putter back a little way, bending the wrists slightly. If you do not bend the wrists then you will stroke the ball, if you bend them fully you will tap the ball. So bend them slightly, and take the head of the putter back, keeping it close to the ground. I have seen very few really good putters who lift the head of the putter well clear of the ground. If you do that you cannot be certain that you are going to strike the ball at right angles to the line. There should be a short follow-through. The head of the putter should not be taken back too far before hitting the ball because that increases the chance of making errors and you want to avoid that on the putting green.

The putting stroke should never be hurried. It is hard to be un-hurried when you feel that you have to hole this one in order to win that half-crown, but the chances are that is just when you will miss it. I like to think of the putting stroke having a certain amount of rhythm. I know that with myself, when I have lost that rhythm, my putting is not what I would like it to be. I think you can best get that sense of rhythm if you stand close to the ball with the head well over it.

I think one of the worst mistakes that golfers make on the putting greens is that they contrive to open the face on the backswing. That means that when it hits the ball it will not be at right angles and the ball will go off on the wrong direction.

So much then for the physical part of putting, what of the mental side? I suppose it is true to say that more short putts are missed because of nerves than because of any other reason. There is not a great deal I can say about that. A state of nerves is something that is peculiarly individual. No two people are alike in that respect. Obviously those who can drill themselves to be calm under all strains and stresses are less likely to be nervous over a putt than those who can't. But I have known some of the most calm people in their respective spheres—surgeons and the like—who have been as nervous as kittens when asked to hole a yard putt for the match.

As far as professionals go, we all suffer from nerves on the greens. That comes mostly after you have several hard tournaments, or when you are struggling to get back your form which has temporarily deserted you.

Experience is the best thing to overcome green-nerves, and it is very rarely that you find a middle-aged golfer who has played the game pretty well for years and years suffering from nerves on the green.

But if you lose your putting touch, keep calm about it. If you reach the state that you can't get the putter off the ground because of nerves then leave the game alone for a bit. If you have just lost putting form, then persevere with the method that has stood by you in the past. Don't panic, don't start experimenting with this grip and that grip, and above all don't go about changing your putters every day. The chances are you'll finish up a nervous wreck and when you recover you will go back to your first putter and your original style!

GETTING OUT OF BUNKERS

FOR some reason or another bunkers terrify golfers, and the very sight of a big bunker some hundred yards ahead is a signal for them to go straight in, with the result that one or perhaps more shots are lost.

Some bunkers are very nasty, particularly on seaside courses, and these great yawning caverns can cause you an enormous amount of trouble. But they need not worry you unduly, for I can assure you that with practice, except for the times when your ball is lying up against the face of the bunker or in a heel-mark, you can get out of every bunker with one stroke. More than that, it is possible on quite a number of occasions to put the ball near the pin if the bunker is at the side of the green. This is a stroke which the Americans have perfected to such an extent that when I am playing one of them and see him go into a bunker at the green, I wish he had been anywhere else either on the green or off it.

Let me say at this point that there is no secret of this success. The Americans have perfect bunker play because they have practised it so often off the course. Then again many of their circuits are heavily bunkered so that they have plenty of opportunities of getting out. Their aim is not only to get out but to get the ball near enough to the flag as to get down in one putt.

It is too much to expect that any average golfer can do that all the time. If he could he would not be an average golfer, but as I say, it is possible to get out in one stroke providing there is a firm intention to get out. I say that because here again in bunker play so many golfers are timid. They are afraid they will knock the ball over the green. That can happen, but I should say that for every time a ball is knocked from a bunker over the green that six shots are either left in the sand or are short, well short, of the hole. Confidence is a great asset when you are playing a bunker. Confidence and the grim determination that the ball is going out of the sand at all costs.

The first important thing about bunker play is to have a club which has been made for the task. In the old days the golfers had to do the best they could with a mashie iron or niblick, or some other club with comparatively little loft. I was never privileged to see any of the great players of the past in their hey-day, but I can imagine

48

that they must have thrown away a good many shots in bunkers; though when one examines their scores they must have been adept enough with the weapons at their disposal.

We have come a long way since those days and now every golf set includes a suitable club for bunker play. If you do not possess a full set of clubs—and there is no disgrace in that—you can always buy a blaster. I would suggest to you that if you do not own one you should take steps to do so right away. I say without any fear of contradiction that the blaster, even if used but moderately well, knocks strokes off the round of even the humblest rabbit. There are some golfers who never learn to get out of bunkers and so have hung a millstone round their necks for all time.

I have suggested earlier that there is no reason to be scared of bunkers. Going into one is a misfortune, I know, but it is not the end of everything. Anyhow, there is nothing you can do about it once you are in. The only thing to do is to try to get out—and get out in one stroke.

First thing to remember is that when your ball is lying in a bunker it may be the result of a thoroughly bad shot. That being so, you step into the bunker in a not too relaxed frame of mind, and then there is a tendency to "have a go" without giving sufficient thought to the shot. That is very wrong. As with other golf strokes you cannot expect results unless you are relaxed, and so if you are feeling just a little mad with yourself just wait a moment and calm down.

Having done that the next thing is to make up your mind on what you are trying to achieve apart from getting the ball on its way. If near the green, the object is to get the ball on the green and as near to the flagstick as possible. If you are some distance from the green, then the object should be to get the ball on the fairway and, if possible, on a part of the fairway from which you will be able to place your next shot. I mean by that if you are in a bunker on the left-hand side of the fairway, and farther down on the left-hand side there are more bunkers, it is not wise to keep on that side. It is better to try to get the ball over to the other side. But having given that advice, generally speaking if you are a long way from the green the main object should be to get the ball on the fairway—anywhere on the fairway.

First thing you have to guard against when you step into a bunker is the desire to hit the ball out cleanly. It may be that the ball is lying very well and that the sand is wet. In such circumstances you must weigh up the question, and ask yourself, "Is it worth the risk?" Even

(a)   (b)

GETTING OUT OF BUNKERS

The stance, showing the position of the ball in relation to the feet

(a) correct; (b) wrong

if you hit a good shot where will the ball land? Will it reach the green over a hundred yards away? In that case it might be worth while to take a bit of a gamble.

But if you ask yourself where the ball might land and the answer is a hundred yards short of the green, is it not better to get the ball on the nearest part of the fairway and then play a longer club for the next shot?

Hitting the ball cleanly out of a bunker is permissible only in rare circumstances and when the player has thought over all the pros and cons. Otherwise I would say, be perfectly orthodox and don't be led away by some of those old legends about players putting the ball on the green with a brassie (No. 2 wood).

The grip is most important in the playing of bunker shots. I grip the blaster practically at the top of the shaft, but there are differences of opinion about this. Some experts advocate a slightly shorter grip. The only time I shorten my grip is when I am in a little shallow bunker at the very edge of the green. Then I take a shorter grip, but play the ball much nearer the left foot and grip the club firmer with my right hand than with my left. It is a useful little shot this, but it requires practice, so we will say no more about it meantime, and go on to the ordinary bunker shot.

I have said where on the shaft you should grip the club. It should be a firm grip and the right hand should be well over the shaft. I will tell you why. If the right hand is allowed to go under the shaft there is a chance you will take the club back in far too flat an arc. This is just what you don't want. The backswing should be upright and the right hand over the shaft will help that, providing, of course, that you break the wrists early as the club goes up.

Many golfers, when they get into a bunker and play a shot, then execute what might be quite properly called a sand dance. This is quite unnecessary. There should be little or no movement of the feet when playing from a bunker. As for the stance, the feet should be fairly close together and the stance should be open, i.e. the left foot should be drawn back from the intended line of flight. There should be no tension as far as the legs are concerned.

Having taken the club back steeply the next move is to bring it down about a couple of inches behind the ball. This distance may vary according to the conditions; for instance, the sand might be very light and dry and the two inches might be increased a shade. If the sand is heavy then the aiming point might be an inch from the ball. Generally, however, two inches can be used as the slide-rule.

You must hit the sand hard, and having done so then the hands and arms must be carried through and up. There can be no good bunker shot unless that is done.

I have given you some simple instruction on getting out of bunkers, but there are times when something goes wrong. You have been too hurried, you have been aiming at the wrong point or perhaps the ball has been lying in such a spot that you really had no chance of getting it out first time.

If the ball is still in the sand after your first attempt, *don't panic*.

Stifle any desire to rush at the ball and hit it any-old-how. Just take your time, remember all the things you should remember, and try again.

RECOVERY SHOTS

By this time you will have already discovered that there are many golf courses which seem nothing more nor less than great expanses of rough interspersed with trees, gorse, heather and all manner of unpleasant things.

I am afraid it is true that the idea in golf is to keep on the fairway and not get into rough; but there is not a golfer alive who does not sample the rough fairly frequently; I can hear some of you saying "too frequently".

No matter what golf instruction you have you will go into rough— you would not be human if you did not—and I would say at the very outset of this chapter that when you do go into rough the thing to do is to get out as economically as possible. If you go chasing after the bad shot in a temper and slash at the ball, the chances are that it will still be in the rough; so I advise coolness, my friends. That is most essential; in fact, it is the first essential.

It is coolness, for instance, that will enable you to examine the lie thoroughly and if the ball is lying badly to decide whether or not it is playable. Do not attempt to get the ball out of the rough if at the back of your mind there is the gnawing thought: "This ball is really unplayable." If it is unplayable, then lift and drop under penalty. It will probably save you strokes in the long run.

But let us leave the very bad rough at the moment, and deal with a situation when the ball is lying in light rough. First thing to decide is which club you are going to play. If in doubt use the more lofted one and play it exactly as you would play the club from a lie on the fairway, making certain that the face is laid a little open. This will ensure that the ball will go up in the air.

The blow must be a very firm one. Many golfers playing from the light rough are inclined to spare the stroke. This is bad; you must hit the ball crisply. Don't be misled by those theorists who tell you there is no need to hit against the left side. I can tell you if you don't hit against the left side, either from the rough or from the fairway, you will not make much progress at this game of golf. Why I advocate a really hefty blow with the club from light rough is that you have to remember that there is some pretty tough grass in the path of the club, and if the clubhead is not made to move swiftly the clubhead will be impeded.

When playing from light rough it is possible to try for a little distance, but from heavy rough it is a very different question.

If your ball is in heavy rough it is your task to get it to the fairway, and the spot of the fairway to aim at is the spot nearest your ball. Many a match and much money has been lost because a golfer thought he could get distance from long grass. What a mistake that is.

It must be quite obvious to everybody that when the ball is lying in long grass that a very big club must be used to get it out, and that club must be used with some power, indeed with all the power you can muster. But don't waste that power by standing too far away from the ball. Get well up to it with your feet which should be close together firmly on the ground.

Play a proper golf stroke. Don't just take the club back and hack at the ball. That will only increase your blood-pressure.

Of all the hazards on a golf course perhaps the most difficult is heather, so if you play on a course with heather you must treat it with great respect. Many lies in heather are impossible, and you should cut your losses and declare the ball unplayable. On heathery courses bare patches of hard sand are often found. There is no definite advice I can give if you land on one of these patches. Each lie brings its own problems and you must meet them when they come. As a rule the thing to do is to get the ball back on the fairway, but always try to play an orthodox stroke, and an unhurried one at that.

What I have said about heather also applies to bushes. Time and again I have seen even experienced golfers go into the middle of a bush and try to play the ball out. Very often their efforts end in disaster. Not long ago a club golfer I know landed in a bush during a competition and he ran up thirteen for the hole. It was the one bad hole of his round and made him depressed for days.

Apart from getting out of rough, heather and bushes, there are other kinds of recovery shots. The ones you have to play over and round trees. My first advice here is to play safe if you are in any kind of doubt at all. But I suppose that my advice will not be heeded by many, because at heart most golfers like a gamble. They like to play a difficult shot and if it is successful relate the success in the clubhouse bar. That's only natural.

The most spectacular shot is the one over a tree, and if you refuse to allow yourself to become intimidated it is a shot that can be brought off.

Obviously you must use a lofted club because usually this kind of

Using a wood from the rough and trying to force the ball out by brute strength. This is not to be recommended

shot is played when the tree is near the green. If the tree is not near the green then there is possibly a way round. A lofted club it is then, and the club must be played down and through the ball. Because there is a tall obstacle in front of you do not try to scoop the ball in the air; if you play the stroke correctly the loft of the club will do that for you. I take a lot of time to play such shots, and I strongly

Playing an iron from the rough, smoothly and without undue effort

advise you to do the same. I am sorry to harp on this unhurried business, but it will pay you to listen and take heed.

But supposing the tree is not near the green, and there is a chance of your getting good results from a shot played round the tree. Then the chance might well be worth taking. There are two kinds of shots which can be played in the circumstances: a pulled shot or a sliced shot.

Many of you will say at once: "Well, I shouldn't have much difficulty in playing such shots because most of my golf is composed of pulls and slices!" The trouble is that they are not so easy to play when you try to play them.

For the slice, stand with an open stance, i.e. with the left foot drawn well back, and the ball should be a little nearer the left foot than it is for normal strokes. The hands should be placed more on top of the shaft. The result of these moves will be to make the club-head come across the ball from outside to inside, causing the ball to veer away to the right. I forgot to say that you are playing round the left of the tree, but I expect you have gathered that already.

For the intentional pull things are pretty much the opposite. In other words, the stance should be closed and the right hand should be more under the shaft. For some reason or other most golfers find the intentional pull easier to play than the intentional slice.

The only other shot I can think of in connection with trees is the one played from underneath the branches. This is a shot which is what I call "chancy". Results may be good, they may be indifferent, but in any case it is sometimes the only shot which is "on".

A fairly straight-faced iron for this one, a 3 or 4 or perhaps a 5 iron. The face of the club should be closed. That is, it should be facing a little to the left. The ball should be nearly opposite the right foot. Just take your ordinary swing except when the branches will not allow you to do this. Then I cannot advise you. With such shots you are "on your own".

Occasionally you have to punch the ball out—play it out with little or no backswing. In such cases get out on the fairway.

Have a good think before you play such shots and have a few practice swings. They will help you to see how far you can take the club back and also help you to compose yourself.

RECOVERY SHOTS FROM
UNEVEN GROUND

SOME courses are hilly, some are flat, but when we describe the latter as flat we don't quite mean that every time the ball lands the ground around it will be completely level. I don't suppose there are many golf courses which have no hillocks or slopes on them, and that being so we must always be prepared for our ball lying on a downward slope, an uphill slope, or on the side of a little mound.

Seaside courses in particular have many slopes, and as such courses are usually dry you will often find when you go up to your ball that it is lying very close. That means there is not much grass on the spot, and as a consequence the shot will not be easy. Such shots should be played with great care, and it is always advisable to take a more lofted club than you would take if the ball were lying on lush grass.

There are four kinds of shots you can expect on slopes: (1) An uphill lie when the ball is lying on the upward slope of the ground. (2) A downhill lie when the ball is lying on the downward slope of the ground. (3) When you have to stand above the ball. (4) When you have to stand below the ball.

Each of these shots has to be played quite differently, and none of them are easy because it is so easy to go off the line from any of the lies I have mentioned. That is the main danger, although it is also very easy especially from a downhill lie to fluff the ball completely.

Let us start with uphill lies, because of all the lies you might get from even ground they are probably the easiest. The question of which club to select is the first problem here. Just think to yourself for a moment which club the distance demands. After deciding that, then take out of your bag a club one size down the scale. In other words, if the distance requires a 4 iron use a 3 iron. The reason for this is that the slope of the ground will make the ball get up in the air to a greater extent than when played off level ground.

As to the position of the ball in relation to the feet for long shots the ball should be in a central position half-way between the feet. For short shots the ball should be farther back to a point almost opposite the right toe.

If the slope is fairly steep there is a tendency to fall back in playing short strokes, so make certain that when the club is brought down all the weight is on the left foot. If it isn't you will stagger back, and it is almost certain that the result of the stroke will be nothing like what you had anticipated.

For long-handicap players I should advise aiming a little to the right when playing off an uphill slope because the slope of the ground has the effect of causing the body to turn more than it should with the result the ball is pulled, or in other words goes to the left. You can also counteract a pull by making sure that the hands are brought right through after the ball is struck.

The stroke from a downhill lie is much more difficult, or at least more modest golfers seem to have more trouble with it. Just as I said that you take one club down the range for uphill lies, so do you take a club one up the scale for a stroke from a downhill lie. If the club you have first in mind is a 4 iron then take a 5 iron. This will make certain that you get the ball in the air. If the downhill lie is quite steep then you may have to use a club even more lofted, for the main thing to bear in mind is not to fluff the stroke. I am sorry if all this sounds a little cautious, but it is better to be on the safe side.

In addition to taking a more lofted club the stance must be open: you remember the expression, which means that the left foot is drawn back. This will help you to take the club back at a steeper angle than usual which is what is required if the ball is to be sent on its way.

Be sure that you do not jab at the ball in a hurried sort of a way because if you do the odds are that the ball will go scuttling along the ground, which is not the object of the exercise.

Now we come to the lies where you are either standing above the ball or below it. First the one where you are standing above the ball. If you are not careful with this there is a chance that you might slice the ball into trouble on the right-hand side of the course. Don't do as I have heard of some players doing—stand for a pull and hope to bring the ball round. No! Aim to the left of the target, making sure that you bring the hands through as fast as you can. When I say "hands" I mean "hands". I do not mean that you should lunge at the ball with all your body. For this shot try to maintain a good balance because good balance is the keynote of all strokes from uneven lies.

When you are playing a stroke from a position below the ball, what you have to be careful of is a pull. It is the easiest thing in the world to heave your shoulders round and send the ball away to the

AN UPHILL LIE

The wrong way. Leaning too far back. Too much weight on the right foot

Weight on the left foot and generally well down to the ball

59

A DOWNHILL LIE

The correct address, easy and natural

Knees too bent, hands too far forword

STANDING ABOVE THE BALL

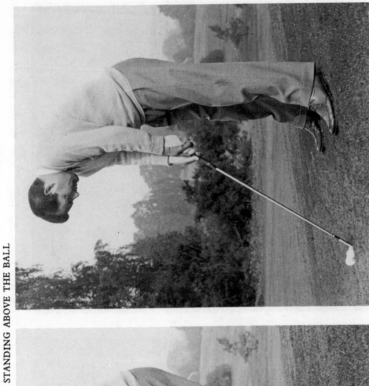

The correct stance with knees bent

The wrong stance. Knees are stiff and there is too much tenseness

STANDING BELOW THE BALL

An easy stance with no strain. Note the hands are a little way down the shaft

Too far from the ball. Hands at the end of shaft. Too tense

left where there are some trees, bushes or a bunker. Some people use an open stance at this one, but I think that it can be dangerous unless you are quite expert. I should advise you to aim to the right of the target. If the slope is very steep then you will have to use an open stance. Again, there should be no falling back when you are playing the stroke.

All over, what is most necessary when playing strokes from uneven lies is to use your common sense. In time you will soon be able to find out for yourself exactly how to stand for each kind of stroke, and I must tell you here and now that you will make many mistakes when playing them.

They must never be hurried. Hurrying the stroke is bad at all times, but especially when you are playing from sloping lies, because there is not much room for error. On the other hand, do not allow yourself to become intimidated by such lies. They are by no means impossible, and you will find that in time you will get good results.

PART TWO — *Common Faults*

TOPPING

A TOP is the most humiliating shot in golf, especially if done off a crowded first tee on a Sunday morning. After carefully taking up your stance, you swing at the ball, hit it hard on the top, and to the great amusement of your friends the ball trickles all along the ground for about thirty yards.

It is very common among long-handicap golfers and beginners. Rarely does it happen to the good player.

What causes a top? Tension certainly, which in turn makes one jerk the head up; and swaying.

Jerking the head up is usually known as "looking up", but there is a difference. The damage will not be too terrible if the golfer simply turns his head to the left at impact. Many good players do this, and it does not bother them because the body does not move when the head turns.

Damage is really done when the movement of the head causes the shoulders to jerk up and turn left at the same time. This makes the clubhead come up and the ball is topped. Yes, it is just as simple as that.

The cure for all this is to make sure your swing is smooth and relaxed.

How can we stop the shoulders jerking up? As I have explained, the slight movement of the head is not really the cause, for the head often moves without affecting the shoulders. But if the shoulders move, the head will follow.

The player who jerks his shoulders will have hit from the top of the swing. His whole hitting action will have collapsed, and in a desperate effort to make the ball go any distance at all he heaves his shoulders at the ball with a lifting motion of the body. This is often caused by tension. Therefore one way to cure it is to concentrate on swinging smoothly. Be especially careful when you have a shot over a pit or ravine when the chances of jerking always seem to be greater.

Many players simply won't believe they jerk up and move the head at impact. If you are one of these, then I suggest you get a friend to help you.

He should stand in front of you with his feet just out of range of your clubhead, and then place his right hand on your head and hold it firm. When you swing you will find that your head jerks out of your friend's hand, and if that isn't good enough I don't know what is.

The second cause of topping is swaying. The lowest part of the swing is at the impact position. If you move this arc a few inches to the right you hit behind the ball, and the clubhead hits the ball above its centre and causes a top.

The cure is to stop the sway. This can only be done by great effort on the golfer's part. First make sure you are swaying. Many golfers think they do sway when in fact they do nothing of the sort. Again a friend can help by watching you, especially if you line up your head with a tree or bush behind you. Then he can see quite easily whether your head moves to the right when you reach the top of the backswing. If it does, then you are swaying.

Having decided that you do sway, the only way to cure it is by forcing yourself not to sway. This may sound ridiculous, but a sway is something with which no one can help you. It is not like a bad grip or a wrong foot movement, which a professional can correct. No, the sway can only be cured by hard work on the golfer's own part.

The third reason for topping, and perhaps the most common among beginners, is the raising of the arc of the swing. The arc is raised on the backswing so that the shoulders and hands are higher at the top of the backswing than they should be. This is caused by dipping the left shoulder on the backswing which throws everything up in the air. Too much weight is on the left foot so that when the player swings down again he falls back on the right foot.

To cure this, first check your address position. Chances are that you are leaning over too far. The body should be bent as little as possible. When you take up the address position bend to the ball by bending the knees slightly. The back should not bend very much.

If a player bends sharply at the waist, the chances are good that he will straighten up as he takes the clubhead back, and once the arc is raised in this way it is extremely difficult to lower to the same point. The result? Yes, you have guessed it. A top.

It is easy to see that if you do reach the top of the backswing with the left shoulder and left knee dipped the weight is on the left leg, and the only place for it to go on the down-swing is on the right leg. This raises the right side sharply and causes a hook.

A swing like this causes the clubhead to be taken back in a narrow arc and to be chopped down on the ball.

Do you think you are a chopper? If you are not sure there is one

Standing too far behind the ball and leaning too far back will
cause topping

quick way of finding out. Go and swing a club in a semi-rough. It
you are swinging it correctly it should brush the grass for about six
inches before it reaches the ball. If it doesn't then you are coming
down too steeply, which will mean that you are lifting the club up
rather than swinging it back.

Therefore you can see that there are many causes of topping and
if you do it persistently then the best advice I can give you is that
you should visit your professional. He will be able to decide quickly
what is causing your top and set about curing it. But remember, it
is no good going to him unless you are prepared to practise what he
tells you.

67

PULLING

THE pull is an infuriating shot. The ball appears to be hit quite well, but instead of going straight down the fairway it goes speeding out to the left and ends up in the rough, making a second shot very difficult.

Now you may think that there is nothing very much wrong with your swing when you pull. After all the ball goes straight. But you can take it from me that there is something very wrong indeed, and it is that you are swinging from outside to in.

You see the pull and the slice are related. Both are caused by the outside-to-in swing. The slice occurs when you hit the ball with the open face and the pull when it is closed. It is just as simple as that. In other words, the clubface is square not to the line of flight but to the line the clubhead is following—to the left.

Anyhow the outside-to-in swing is one of the worst faults in golf. If the worst that happens is a pull, quite frankly you are lucky.

Now for the cure. The trouble with the outside-to-in swing is that the position at the top of the backswing is all wrong. This means that the first movement of the down-swing is often bad, and when they are combined, disaster strikes.

To reach the correct position at the top of the swing it is vital that the first movement should be correct. I can't stress that too strongly. Take the clubhead back all in one piece with the shoulders, arms, hands and club moving together. This movement insures that you go back on the inside groove after the first few inches of the swing. If the club starts back on the outside it will be impossible to reach the right position at the top of the swing, so you can see how important this first take-away movement is to good golf.

At the top of the swing there are a number of points to check. There should be more weight on the right foot than on the left, and the head must be fixed. It is no earthly use doing everything else correctly if you sway to the right. The shoulders must be turned to a full ninety degrees and the right wrist must be under the shaft.

It is important that more weight be on the right foot at the top of the swing. If it is on the left one it will shift automatically on to the right at the start of the down-swing. This in turn throws the right hip and hands forward and to the right, which means everything will be outside the intended line and an outside-to-in swing is the only possible result.

If the golfer sways the whole swing is moved back in that direction. On the down-swing the club comes down a little on the right. The sway also means that the pivot is restricted, for many golfers imagine that they have pivoted beautifully when all they have done in fact is to sway badly. The sway also means that the club will not be straight and pointing to the hole at the top of the backswing. Also, because the whole swing has moved to the right the clubhead will in fact be travelling at its fastest before it hits the ball, and the tendency will be that it will be closing when at last it does make impact, causing a pull.

The full turn of the shoulders is vital because if the pivot is restricted the body usually turns sharply to the left at the start of the down-swing, throwing hands and club outside the line and causing a pull or a slice, but if the clubhead is held square a pull.

The right wrist must be under the shaft so that the left hand is strong at the top of the swing, making the naturally stronger right hand weaker. This stops the golfer hitting early for it is the right hand that does the damage when we hit early. By keeping it under the shaft it can't overpower the left hand. If you do not get it in the right position the chances are that it will take over and throw everything outwards, causing an outside-in swing, just the thing we are trying to avoid.

Well, that has cleared up the position at the top of the backswing, and if you are not clear about it now, then I suggest a visit to your professional is overdue.

Now to the other cause of a pull, the first movement of the down-swing. This should be a movement of the hips to the left. The hands and arms stay still. By moving the hips you will move the rest of the body round and in turn the hands and arms will follow, but the movement must not be started by the hands and arms. That is most important and one of the most important factors in hitting a golf ball.

When the hands and arms do begin to move keep the wrists cocked as long as possible and at least until the hands reach the level of your waist. From this position the hands throw the clubhead at the ball. From there it will be impossible for them to move on an outside-to-in plane. Yes, you will have hit from the inside and everything will be fine. However, if the hands take control too early, everything will be thrown out of gear and you will hit from outside to in.

SHANKING

THE very mention of the word shank makes me shudder. It is without doubt the most soul-destroying fault in golf and nothing is calculated to break a golfer's heart more quickly.

I know some of my fellow professionals who will not even contemplate giving a pupil a lesson if his fault is shanking. You may think it strange that any professional should turn down money like this but the reason is simple. A shank—the shot where the ball goes off the join of the shaft and the clubhead at any angle except the intended one—is the most terrifying one in golf. It strikes without warning, often in the middle of a good round. From the moment a golfer shanks, he becomes a different man. From the easy, happy-go-lucky golfer of a moment before he becomes a shaking jelly of a man unable to explain why he finds it difficult to hit the ball.

What causes a shank? In the case of the professional refusing to give a lesson, he thought that even watching someone who could do it might start him off as though he had caught a contagious disease; but the real cause is that the golfer who shanks swings with an exaggerated outside-to-in swing with very little pivot and a very loose wristed action.

The swing is so much on the outside that the clubhead never makes contact with the ball as it is entirely outside the ball. The only part of the club that can hit the ball is the shank. If you are not sure whether you have hit a shank or not, just look at the shaft after the shot. Then you will see the tell-tale little white mark on it where the ball has hit and the paint has come off.

A good swing hits the ball straight, but the swing which causes a shank is terrible, and the only way to put it right is to start all over again and check practically every position and movement.

Two main things cause a shank. In the first the golfer starts back more or less on the inside line, but bends back his wrists very quickly. This causes a restricted pivot so that at the top of the swing he throws the club to the outside. The clubhead actually makes a big loop from the inside to the outside and, of course, the ball is hit on the shank. The second is when the golfer takes the clubhead back from the ball on the outside and then makes a quick throw from the top. This one is even worse than the first but both are frightening.

These photographs show two reasons for shanking a shot

In the first photograph the club face has been turned back and the swing is flat

In the second photograph the wrists are being rolled in the opposite direction

So to make a cure let's start from the beginning. Start the back-swing all in one piece and transfer the weight from the left foot to the right. Keep the left arm fairly straight. Those people who say it should be like a ramrod are talking nonsense. Turn the shoulders the full ninety degrees and keep the right wrist under the shaft.

Now most good golfers do all these things, but they still shank occasionally. Why? The answer is tension and anxiety.

The shank is almost bound to happen when a golfer starts playing well and then suddenly becomes over-anxious; and no one is going to tell me that this has not happened to them at some time or other. I know it sometimes happens to me, and it is then that I have to work really hard to keep my swing going. How many of you start trying to steer the ball when this happens? Most of you, I've no doubt, and when you do you are leaving yourselves wide open for a shank.

The reason is that when a golfer starts to play carefully, or as he thinks cannily, he shortens his backswing and restricts his pivot without realising it. This makes him swing just a little on the outside. The result is a pull. The golfer starts to worry. What is causing this sudden pull? Then he makes a great effort to keep it straight, and before he can say "Ryder Cup" he has shanked. In fact, his pivot is so restricted, his wrist action so quick and loose and his swing so much on the outside, that he is lucky to hit the ball at all.

Keen golfers will have noted from this that the warning sign that a shank is lurking just round the corner is the pull. This is the red light, as it were, and so if you start to pull that is the moment to take your swing in hand and say to yourself: "I'm not going to allow this to become a shank."

Now a word of warning to you golfers who fancy yourselves as cut shot specialists. I know it looks very good when it comes off and that your friends admire a shot which stops quickly. But take my advice: keep off this type of shot unless you are a really good player. Thinking yourself an expert cut shot artist is the first step to becoming a first-class shanker.

When the average golfer plays these cut shots he opens the face and swings farther and farther from the outside until suddenly, one day, he shanks. Some people may think they don't play these shots like this at all, but take it from me they do and the results in the end are nearly always disastrous. So leave these shots well alone. They are really for professionals only. But you won't find many of the profes-sionals trying them unless they have to; for one thing about a shank is that it can strike at all types of golfers, and, as I have said, the only way to make a real cure is go back to the beginning. Go down to the practice ground and work hard at making a good swing.

I expect you have noticed that most people shank on the little shots around the green. This is because they are tensed up and are trying to steer the ball in the manner I have explained. A good golfer never allows his swing to become restricted and tense. He may be tense inside, but he has confidence in his swing. He knows that he has practised it and he knows that it will work automatically in a crisis. It is when a golfer can start thinking in this confident way that he is really beginning to get somewhere in this game.

PUSHING

IF you have played golf for any length of time, you will know the push shot only too well. It is the one where the ball flies straight off to the right of the target. It does not curve away like a slice and most golfers do not realise they have hit a bad shot. They just assume they were aiming in the wrong direction.

The pushed shot is a bad one, but it can be cured quite easily, for a golfer who pushes the ball out has one thing in his favour. He must be swinging with an inside-to-out swing and, as I have said many times, that is a good thing. The push is caused because the clubhead is slightly open at impact when the club is still travelling from inside to out.

Why is it open? There are a number of answers to this question, but the most common is because the body is ahead of the ball when it is struck, in other words the golfer has swayed into the ball. This means that the body is ahead of the hands as they come into the hitting area and the hands are given no chance to do their work—to whip the clubhead through. The hands just can't be made to work that fast and they have no chance of getting the clubhead square at impact.

What happens is that the hands get the clubhead into the right position a fraction of a second after the ball has been hit because the forward sway has moved the whole arc of the swing to the right. The effect is exactly the same as if the golfer had played his usual swing, but had moved the ball back a few inches towards the right foot. There again the clubhead would reach the ball before it had been brought square to the line by the action of the hands.

As the whole trouble is caused by the sway, let us find out what causes a golfer to move like this. There are two main causes. A sway to the right as the backswing is made and a jerk up of the head.

This pulling up of the head is a very common fault and it would be quite all right if the only thing golfers lifted were their heads; but unfortunately when a player lifts his head quickly he usually jerks up his head and body, and that is no good. In fact, it is bad because it gets the body and hands ahead of the ball at impact and, as I have stressed, one of the secrets of good golf is that the hands should lead the clubhead throughout the swing.

No professional can stop you lifting your head. Keeping it down is something which you have just got to force yourself to do. One tip I can give you is to keep looking at the spot where the ball was until your right shoulder comes underneath and forces your head up. Then the ball will be well on its way to the target and there will have been no suspicion of a head-up. Chances are too that the ball will be going straight.

The sway to the right as one goes back is something which must be avoided at all costs, for most golfers realise that they have swayed when they get to the top and in a tremendous effort to put things right sway back again to the left and overdo it. Then they get their body and hands in front of the ball. The way to stop this is to keep your head still. As I have said elsewhere, the head is the centre point of the swing and it should hardly move at all while the swing is made. Everything should revolve round it. If it is kept still then you can take it from me the body will not move and there will be no reason to put anything right for everything will be going smoothly as you swing.

I have written about swaying in a previous chapter using a friend and a bush! He (the friend) will be able to see very easily indeed whether you move. You can also see for yourself by swinging in front of a mirror at home; but make sure there is enough room to take a full swing or you might be in trouble with your wife, especially if she is a non-golfer and doesn't understand the problem!

Some golfers may find that they have a combination of a sway and a jerk with the head. This will account for a very bad push or a push which develops into a slice.

Another reason for pushing is a swing which, although inside-to-out, is flat. This is usually caused by a quick rolling of the wrists as the clubhead is taken away from the ball. This in turn causes the clubface to be open at the top of the swing, and once that has happened the golfer, unless he is very lucky, rarely gets it closed or even square again by the time he hits the ball. However, as the swing has been fairly good he does not slice, but the open face causes the shot to fly straight out to the right.

The cure for this is to take the clubhead away all in one piece, to make sure you do not roll the wrists open. That's all there is to it, and really that is not so very difficult, is it?

The last thing which I want to mention which causes a pushed shot has nothing to do with the swing at all. With the most perfect swing you can still push if you position the ball in the wrong place, i.e. too near your right foot. By doing this you have naturally brought the body ahead of the ball and the effect is the same as if you had swayed to the right.

When the ball is teed up too much to the right the clubhead has no chance at all of getting square at impact. It is open when the ball is hit and the ball flies out to the right. This is so simple that many people tend to forget it; so the next time you find yourself continually pushing the ball out to the right of the target just check the position at which the ball is teed up. This may be causing all the trouble and you will not have to start messing about with your swing.

HOOKING

If you hook, then you are well on the way to becoming a good golfer. And I am not trying to be funny. That is a fact, for the hook is by no means the worst fault in golf, but it can be the most annoying thing to someone who plays quite well.

It rarely troubles the very long-handicap players, and therefore if you find a hook creeping into your game, don't panic.

I say this with great confidence because it is very difficult to hook with an outside-to-in swing and that is the swing of the bad player. If you hook, the chances are that your swing is inside-to-out, and that is just fine.

But any golfer who wants to improve and become really good will be just as keen to get rid of a hook as he is to eliminate any other fault.

The basic cause of the hook is that the clubface is closed at the moment of impact. Just so that you can see the position for yourselves take a club and lay the clubhead behind the ball as in the address. Now roll your wrists slightly to the left. The clubhead turns. The toe goes in and the loft on the clubface is reduced. That is the position of the clubhead at impact when you hook. The clubhead is no longer at right angles to the line of flight. It is turned to the left.

If you hit the ball with the clubhead like this with an outside-to-in swing—the old slicer's swing—then the ball will go to the left. It may fade at the end but it won't hook. More likely the ball will go straight out to the left and the shot will be a pull which is no use to anyone.

On the other hand, if the swing is inside-to-out the ball will go to the right, then curve in to the left.

Now what causes the clubface to arrive at impact in a closed position? Almost certainly it will have been closed at the top of the backswing, and there are two main reasons for this. The first is a bad grip and the second is a bad backswing. So let us check both of them.

First the grip. I have already described the correct grip, but if you are hooking, then these are the points to look out for. Is the left hand too much on top of the shaft—in other words, are more than two knuckles of the left hand showing? If they are that is wrong. Second, is the right hand too much under the shaft? It is a very common fault to let it slip round and this can prove fatal. Check this position and remember that the V made by the forefinger and thumb should point over the right shoulder not way outside it.

Unfortunately if one hand is in the wrong position the other almost always follows suit and gets into the wrong place.

The reason this grip causes a hook is that it closes the clubface as it turns the wrists to the right out of their natural position.

If you don't believe me check it for yourself. Address the ball again with the wrong grip. Look at the clubhead, see how it is closed and that is what happens when you swing with this wretched grip. At the top of the backswing the clubface will be closed. In other words, the clubface will point to the sky and when you come down it will still be closed and only a hook can result.

So check your grip thoroughly. I assure you that it is more often than not the cause of a hook, and it is so easy to put right.

What about the second cause of a hook? The backswing. This is more serious but don't despair. With a little thought it can be put right. Usually those golfers who hook with a good grip either swing much too flat or pick the club up too quickly with the right hand.

Here we have the hands of a hooker. Right hand too far under, left hand too much on top

By a flat swing I mean that the left arm swings round the body. This again causes the clubface to be closed at the top of the swing.

Most flat swingers begin their swings by rolling the wrists to the right and then swinging round. When they come down they have to try to roll the wrists closed again at the moment of impact. Then the

77

trouble starts. They overdo it and then roll them too far and the ball goes off in a vicious hook.

So when you start the backswing make sure you do not roll the wrists open. Take the clubhead back square to the line of flight and all in one piece. Keep the clubhead, the hand and wrists in line and delay the cocking of the wrists.

The quick pick-up with the right hand is a very common fault. Most people are right-handed and their right hands are stronger than their left hands. The right hand tends to dominate the swing. Immediately a hooker starts his swing you will see the right hand take over and pick up the club and throw it over the right shoulder. Once again this causes the clubhead to be closed at the top of the swing.

What causes the quick pick-up? Many things, but the chief ones are lack of confidence and ignorance of the golf swing.

I cannot cure your lack of confidence, but I can put you right on the swing. Most important when fighting this right-hand domination is once again to remember to go back all in one piece.

Although golf is a two-handed game I repeat that many long-handicap golfers would be well advised to grip the club slightly more firmly with the left hand. Better still, work at strengthening the left hand. Make it as strong as the right one. Swing a heavy club with the hand for a few minutes each day and you'll be surprised how soon it becomes stronger.

To recap: check your grip, the start of the backswing and the position of the clubface at the top of the backswing; if these positions and movements are correct then you can forget about hooking.

What about hooking at will? This is easy but I cannot stress too strongly that these refinements are really for the better players. If you are a long-handicap player leave them well alone for you will only get in a terrible muddle.

To hook at will one only has to put the right hand more under the shaft and close the stance—move the left foot forward—and then swing. You will then hook. Controlling it is more difficult and the best players do it through their hands. Once again you can see how important strong hands are to good golf.

SLICING

To slice is easy. It's the straight ones which are difficult to hit. I should say that nine out of ten people who take up the game develop a slice. There is no doubt about it: slicing is the most common fault in golf.

Some people who have a slice simply despair and get over it by aiming off to the left of the fairway and hoping the ball will drift back into the middle. Others just give the game up. To do either of these is ridiculous, for once you understand why you slice a cure is quite simple.

First of all there are two types of slice: the one which happens every time, and the one which breaks out only occasionally and wrecks what would otherwise be a good score.

Generally the longer-handicap players come into the first class, so I will deal with them first.

These "every time" slicers send the ball out to the right because their hit is with an outside-to-in swing. That is, the clubhead goes away from the body on the backswing and then in an effort to correct it the club is brought back across the ball, putting spin on to the ball at impact. The whole secret in curing this is to reach the correct position at the top of the swing, so let me run over the position for you.

At the top of the backswing there should be more weight on the right foot than the left. The shoulders should be turned ninety degrees and the hips forty-five degrees. The left arm is reasonably straight, the right elbow points down.

The grip with the left hand is firm and the right wrist is under the shaft. The club itself points across the line of flight, in other words at the green.

Check this position, and if you are not absolutely sure that it is right get your professional to have a look at it for you.

Once you are in the right position at the top of the backswing it is much more difficult to slice, but it is easy to drift back into bad habits and there is one quick check to find out whether you are still swinging from outside to in.

Tee up a ball and then put another tee in the ground above five inches to the left of the ball and just over three inches inside the direction line. Now hit the ball. If you are swinging from outside to in the second tee will be moved. If you are swinging correctly you will not touch it.

Then there is another way to check up. Make sure of your follow-through position. If your hands have swung round quickly to the left and finished near your right shoulder you have swung from outside to in. But if your hands have followed the ball, as they will do in a correct swing, then everything is all right.

This, then, is the way to straighten up the habitual slice. Make sure you are in the correct position at the top of the backswing and then swing down as I have told you in another chapter. Beware of letting your shoulders take control, for this too can cause the club to be moved out of line.

Now what about the people who only slice once in a while? The root of this evil is hitting the ball with the clubface open at impact. This is the answer whether the swing has been outside-to-in or inside-to-out. The only exception being the push shot, a ball hit straight to the right of the target. This occurs because the body sways into the ball. However, do not get a push mixed up with a slice, so unless you are certain that you are pushing, forget it.

The slice which occurs only occasionally is easy to spot, for the ball usually starts straight enough but then fades away quite sharply at the end.

In setting out to beat this kind of slice, first check your grip. Make sure that two knuckles of the left hand are showing and that your right hand is not too far on top of the shaft.

If your grip is wrong then the clubface will be open at the top of the swing, which will cause the trouble at impact. The clubhead may be travelling along a straight line, but because the clubface is open the ball will be hit with spin and will slice.

Now this type of slice usually attacks the better players, but there is one certain method of getting rid of it, and that is by playing with what is known as the square-faced method. Most of the top Americans use this; it is very simple and I thoroughly recommend it. It is simply keeping the clubface square to the ball throughout the swing and eliminating that last minute roll of the wrists at impact. In other words, if you open the clubface on the backswing, you'll have to close it again on the way down—unless you get the timing just right you are going to be in trouble; and it is easy to see that if you are a little late getting the clubface square to the ball, then you will hit with an open face and slice. Therefore take the club away square and keep it square throughout the swing. Keep the wrist position firm at impact and then you should get the hang of it.

This is the slicer's grip all right. The right hand is much too far over the shaft and the left hand is too far under

One final word of warning about a slice. Don't try to correct it as you are playing a round by messing about with your grip and your stance. Any fool can cure it by putting the right hand under the shaft and by closing the stance, but this only develops another fault and is no good at all.

No, if you want to really get rid of your slice—and let's face it, your golf won't improve much until you do something about it—then the place to work at it is on the practice ground.

Go down to your practice ground and decide which kind of slice you have and then follow the points I have mentioned. Practise hard and you should find that your slice will disappear.

SKYING

NOTHING looks more ridiculous than a golfer who skies the ball. After a tremendous effort he hits the ball an almighty wallop, nearly falling over at the same time and the ball just sails up into the air as though it is going to beat the altitude record and then comes crashing down again about 100 yards away with very little achieved for an enormous effort.

This can be particularly annoying if it has been raining, and nobody is going to tell me this is a rare occurrence in this country, for the ball is apt to get itself plugged in the wet ground when it comes down again. This makes the next shot very difficult indeed.

The skied shot is really the exact opposite to the top. When you top the ball you hit it half-way up. When you sky it too much of the clubface is below the ball.

What causes a skied shot? The most common reason is a forward lunge and a chop. When this happens the chances are the club has been lifted too steeply on the backswing and most of the weight has moved on to the right leg. From this spot the wretched golfer tries to hit the ball. How he thinks he will ever succeed I just do not know. Anyhow, he brings the club and his weight down together. The body lunges to the left and the hands are well ahead of the clubhead at impact with the result that the ball is hit just behind and at a sharp angle. The club hits the ground and the ball at the same moment, but unfortunately contact with the ball is not made with the clubface but with the top of the club. You can easily see whether you are doing this by examining your club when you start skying. Almost certainly you will see the tell-tale little white marks where the paint has come off the ball as you have hit it.

To stop skying, we must work out a swing that will bring the clubhead along its proper path, parallel to the ground instead of coming down too sharply. This chopping motion is really caused by a wrong movement very early in the swing. In fact, things will start to go wrong with the very first movement. A golfer who skies the ball will almost certainly have lifted the club too steeply. When he tries to hit he will then bring it down too steeply and that is the cause of the trouble. The cure is our old friend the take-away at the start of the swing. I cannot stress too many times that this must be done with the clubhead, arms and wrists all in one piece, all in a straight line. The wrists can start to bend back quite quickly, but for the first foot or so of the swing the whole thing should be in one piece. At the same time the weight should be shifted to the right foot, and it will be there at the top of the swing so that it can be transferred easily to the left foot on the downswing. Taking the club away in one piece will eliminate any suggestion of a quick lift back. Rather the club will be swung back correctly and it will be almost impossible to chop down on the ball. So you can see that it is vitally important that the take-away movement is correct.

However, there is another cause of skying. Yes, many golf faults can be caused by a number of wrong movements in the swing. This one is the turning over of the clubhead. This is often the result of the lunge and the chop.

It is more likely to be caused by that bad habit of rolling the wrists or because the right hand, the stronger one with most golfers, has taken over control.

If the right hand is taking control the position at the top of the backswing will be wrong. The wrists will not be under the shaft as they should be. The answer to this problem is to correct the position at the top of the swing. Make sure that the right wrist is under the shaft. It is also a good idea to set about strengthening the left hand so that the hands can work together.

This can be done by doing exercises or swinging a heavy club. Squashing a rubber ball in the left hand is another good way of making it strong, but the best way is undoubtedly to swing a weighted club with the left hand only. This must be done regularly if it is to be any good at all. You can do it at home. Ten minutes swinging each day will soon bring the left hand up to scratch and it is well worth while. Most good golfers have strong hands and they have made them strong by hard work.

If rolling the wrists is the cause of the trouble then the problem is going to be harder to solve. Chances are that the golfer has been told at some time or another that one must roll the wrists over to play golf well. This is nonsense and it must be stopped. Today nearly every top-class player uses the square-faced method. He takes the clubhead away square to the ball and brings it down in the same way. There is no suggestion of a roll of the wrists, and I am sure this is correct.

Rolling the wrists causes a skied shot when the golfer has rolled the wrists open on the backswing and then overdone the roll back on the way down. When you roll them too far it is impossible to hit the ball with the clubface, and it is hit partly with the top of the clubhead.

One fallacy about skying which I want to kill straight away is that teeing the ball too high always results in a skied shot. It does nothing of the sort. Most tees are not long enough for the clubhead to go under the ball at impact. Therefore, you can't stop skying by simply teeing your ball lower. The cause is deeper than that. People who use a very low tee often sky the ball. I hope I have made it quite clear that there is nothing in that theory.

Therefore, if you sky the ball check the position at the top of the backswing. Don't forget to take the clubhead away in one piece and make sure you have a good full swing. Be careful you do not sway and remember do not roll your wrists. These may sound a lot of things to remember, but you will not be troubled by skying if your swing is correct.

OTHER FAULTS—THE SMOTHER—
THE SCLAFF

GOLF faults are like the weather. Just when you think everything has been cleared up, along comes something else to ruin your game and wreck your nerves. Although many faults result from one cause, few have the same result, but two which are very much alike are the smother and the sclaff. With both the ball does not go very far, in both it goes along the ground, and so if you are one of those unfortunate people who never seem to be able to get the ball into the air take heed of what I am about to say.

First I will deal with the smother. Like so many golf faults it usually occurs when a golfer has a wood in his hand. Just as he is dreaming of the big hit right down the middle, the smother strikes. Instead of sailing away into the clear blue sky the ball dives into the rough on the left of the tee without getting off the ground at all.

The cause is quite simple, but the cure is more difficult. The smother is played when the clubface is hooded at impact. The natural loft of the club is eliminated and it becomes impossible to hit the ball into the air. It must go into the ground.

How far will a smother travel? If you are lucky and have not turned the clubhead too much it may go about 120 yards, but more likely it will dive into the rough about 25 yards from the tee.

To cure it, therefore, we have got to find out what causes the clubface to be hooded at impact, and there are two main reasons. The first is that the grip is wrong and the second is that the position at the top of the backswing is bad.

Both hands can play a part in making the grip wrong. Remember, golf is a two-handed game, and so if either the left or the right hand are too much to the right of the shaft the clubface will be closed at the top of the swing. If this is so, then you don't have to bet on the fact that it will be closed at impact. If this is exaggerated until the clubface is hooded then a smother can be the only result. If the clubface is only slightly shut you will get a hook.

Immediately you take the wrong grip on the club you place a strain on the wrists and especially the left one. The trouble starts when you begin the backswing, because the left wrist will slip back into its natural position and turn the clubhead over. This means that the clubface is shut at the top of the backswing.

Therefore, check your grip. Make sure that only two or two and a half knuckles are showing on the left at address; and when you place the right hand on the club check again the V made by the forefinger and thumb points over the right shoulder. If you adopt this grip you will find that the wrists are in their natural position and they won't turn on the backswing.

A correct grip is absolutely vital is you are to play golf properly. It is the hinge of the whole swing and can make or mar anything which comes after it. The hands are the only part of the body in actual contact with the club and, therefore, it is more than worth while spending a little time checking on the grip. I know that many great players—and in particular Peter Thomson, the magnificent Australian professional—check their grips before they hit every shot. You watch Thomson next time you have the chance and you will see what I mean.

Having got that out of my system, I will now turn to the position at the top of the backswing which causes a smother. The trouble is usually made by the wrists being in the wrong position. If the left wrist is under the shaft the face of the club will almost certainly be opened. Then when the down-swing starts the stronger right hand takes over with a vengeance. Immediately this happens it closes the clubface. If this is so bad that the clubface is hooded, the result will be a smother.

In contrast if the right wrist is under the shaft the right hand will be weakened and the left will be in command. This stops the more powerful right hand from taking charge and closing the clubface and then the worry of a smother evaporates.

A friend can help you cure your smothering. Get him or her to watch your left hand as you swing and particularly at the top of the backswing. He will be able to see whether your fingers open at the top of the swing. If they do, then you must do your utmost to cure it, for this is a very bad fault. The right hand has taken charge and the game has immediately become a one-handed one instead of two-handed.

If these faults, the bad grip and the wrong wrist position at the top of the swing, are combined then you will really have to take yourself off to the practice ground and go to work on curing them. Don't despair, however, for if you follow what I have told you, then you will be able to get rid of a smother.

Although these are the main reasons for smothering there are one or two others which can cause this nasty fault. While you are about it you would be well advised to check that you are pivoting properly and that the shoulders have turned a full ninety degrees on the backswing. The left shoulder may be dipping on the backswing, which will cause bad weight transference when the down-swing is started. The result of this will be a collapse of the left side at impact and a quick smother.

Just to recap then: check your grip, hold on to the club firmly throughout the swing and make sure the wrists are in the right position at the top of the backswing and check the pivot.

Now I want to come to a fault which is not so common. It is sclaffing. It hardly ever attacks a good player, but if you are one of those who find it difficult to break ninety then you will be all too familiar with sclaffing.

Sclaffing is caused by hitting the ground behind the ball and I am afraid it is a difficult fault to cure, for it is caused by so many bad things.

You have no doubt met the confirmed sclaffer, the man who sometimes hits his divot farther than the ball. He describes himself as a golfer, but really he cannot play the game at all.

The first fault which is made by the sclaffer is a quick bend of the left knee at the start of the backswing. This immediately throws the weight transference out of gear, as the weight is thrown on to the left foot instead of the right on the backswing.

To add to the sclaffer's troubles the bending of the left knee means that the left shoulder and the head drop. The head does not maintain its all-important position around which everything revolves. It should not move up and down just as it should not go from side to side when one is swinging a golf club. It should remain still like the hub of a wheel. Many people talk about watching the ball, but I am sure this is not so important as keeping the head still.

The wrong transference of weight will restrict the pivot, and if you don't believe me try it and see for yourself. Move your weight on to the left foot and then try to pivot properly. It's virtually impossible.

This restriction of pivot means that the backswing is abbreviated. The player has already committed so many golfing sins that it is no longer important that his grip and the position of his arms and wrists may be correct. Even if they are he will not have given himself a chance to hit a good ball.

What happens when a sclaffer starts his down-swing? First he begins it from the top. He throws the clubhead, and this spells disaster. Next he thinks about transferring his weight. As it is on the left foot he hurls it on to the right. The combined movement of throwing the club from the top and shifting the weight to the right means that the clubhead comes crashing down behind the ball. Added to this, many players will bend the right knee on the down-swing because they have already bent the left one. This only aggravates the position.

Now for the cure. To anyone who knows anything about golf it is pretty obvious. First the backswing. Start it all in one piece. Yes, I know I have mentioned this many times before, but it cannot be over-emphasised. Take the clubhead away square from the ball. Do not dip the left knee and keep the head still. Let the weight move smoothly on to the right foot as the backswing is made. If this weight transference is done properly there will be no danger of bending the right knee or dropping the head as the down-swing is started. Also there will be little danger of hitting early once the top of the swing position has been achieved correctly. The little danger that does remain of hitting too soon can be completely eliminated if you start the down-swing by turning the hips to the left with no movement of the hands and arms. This will mean that the hands are ahead of the clubhead and it will be impossible to hit too soon.

So you can see that sclaffing can be avoided if the start of the back-swing is made correctly. It is completely useless to try and stop someone sclaffing by picking out just one fault and trying to get him to cure it. The reasons for this fault are very basic and, therefore, he should go right back to the beginning to put it right.

I said at the start of these remarks on sclaffing that it hardly ever affected a good player, and that is true. The only time it does strike them is when they are trying to do something completely different. It happens when they are trying to hit a particularly long ball. I expect you have seen it happen.

The good player faced by a long hole at which he hopes to get on in two decides to go for a big one right down the middle. As he gets ready to hit the ball he drops his right shoulder. His body is no longer vertical. It is curved to the right and more weight is put on the right foot. The player is trying to make sure he hits the ball hard in the back, but I am afraid he is leaving himself wide open for sclaff. What happens? Sometimes he will come down hard behind the ball. Of course this does not happen every time, but it can take place and needs watching.

In these last few chapters I have taken you through the main faults in golf. I have explained what causes them and told you how to cure them. The most important thing to remember about golf faults is that they can be cured by a little hard work and careful thought. Yes, you may think that is obvious, but there are many players who seem resigned to putting up with their faults. If they have a slice they aim off for it, and so on. This is perfectly all right until the player suddenly hits one correctly and it flies in the direction he is pointing and goes on straight instead of curving back into the middle of the fairway. How much less risky it would be to try and work out a formula for hitting the ball straight. No! Golf faults can be cured; and remember if you find yourself completely baffled then a visit to your professional will probably prove well worth while. He can bring an expert eye to bear on your problem. He knows what to look for and can easily and quickly put you back on the road to better and more enjoyable golf.

PART THREE — *Odds and Ends*

THE MENTAL SIDE

THERE are many first-class golfers in the world, men of real class, who can win in the best of company. There are also golfers—and there will be one or more in your club—who have real golfing ability, men who in events of local importance can score like the best professional and who can go round the course in record figures when there is nothing at stake.

But in a national championship or major event they never succeed. They have a run of bad luck, their opponent plays the game of his life, or to use a well-worn phrase "they were never off the fairway but the putts wouldn't drop". These players are kidding nobody but themselves. The reason they never win any big competitions is that their nerves get the better of them when towards the end of the last round or in the semi-final of a championship, they begin to see in the mind's eye a gleaming trophy on their sideboard.

"All that", I can hear some people say, "has nothing to do with me." I am sorry to say it has, for there are many thousands of humble golfers who suffer from nerves; when they are confronted with a four-foot putt to take a half-crown off their opponent, they fail lamentably and shudder in horror or quiver with disappointment as the ball slides past the hole. These are the same people who in the Monthly Medal are "never off the fairway but couldn't get the putts to go down". The same people who playing in the captain's handicap competition come up against an opponent playing the game of his life.

Yes, nerves affect great and small. They cause you to become all tensed up, and the harder you try the less you succeed until in the end your game is a thing of shreds and patches.

There are two sides to golf: the technical side and the mental side. The ideal is to attain such a standard that the technical or mechanical side of the game becomes second nature. In other words, you have to swing the club the same way each time. If you can attain a standard anywhere near that then you can get ready your speech of thanks which winners of prizes at golf competitions must make.

But so few people reach that standard because they are not properly equipped mentally, and in that category I put most amateurs and about seventy-five per cent of professionals. The others are those who are not afraid to win championships and competitions.

If there are really so many golfers who are not properly equipped mentally, it must be suggested that I am fighting a lone crusade and that nothing I can say or write will alter things substantially. Well, that is one point of view, but if the rank and file golfers would only pay attention to what I write and what others have said and written then they would *improve their golf enormously*. Do you want to do that? Presumably you do or you would not be reading this book. All right then; you must get these nerves under control and in general get yourself properly attuned so that you shut out everything else except the job on hand. And always the job on hand in golf is the actual stroke you are playing.

I have said that some golfers fail when they look forward to winning an event. It is also true to say that many fail because they are still thinking of the last shot they have played or perhaps even the bad shot before that. They are worried by that stroke and keep on worrying about it. They are still worrying when they play their next stroke, which is almost certain to be a bad one. I have no need to explain further because it must be obvious to all what happens next.

This forgetting the last bad stroke is a very hard thing to do. When I am playing in a tournament and am thoroughly tuned up I don't find it so hard, but when I am playing in a friendly game then I do find it difficult. I expect you will find it even more difficult, but all the same it is an ideal which you must try to live up to.

If you can forget the bad shots you have played then I feel, too, that you will be relaxed, and that is a very necessary frame of mind to be in if you are to play better golf. Of course there are golfers who are the very opposite of relaxed before they even hit their first tee-shot. I mean the ones who rush from the clubhouse to the first tee—I have mentioned them elsewhere. It is just impossible for them to be relaxed certainly for the first three holes and by that time a lot of damage may be done. Then there are the golfers who get agitated because the players behind are catching up on them. There are others who are agitated because the players in front are holding them up.

Golfers are liable to be upset by all manner of things in addition to the fact that they are playing badly, and this is certainly not conducive to good scoring.

You must never rush to the tee, but should arrive early at the club, change leisurely and you then should really go to the practice ground. I say "should really go" because I know that only a percentage of you will take that advice. Moderate golfers seem to be shy of going to the practice ground at any time, least of all within minutes of playing a round. They are afraid they will be laughed at by their friends. I grant you these friends may make the odd remark or two, but if the result of your practice is that you play well and possibly win your match, why should you worry?

We have decided that two important factors in stopping nerves and getting into the right mood for good golf is (a) to be relaxed and (b) to forget that last shot when you are playing the next.

From there I think we should go on to the vexed question of concentration. You may or may not have read a good many golf books, but I'm sure that at some time or another you have read about the necessity to concentrate when you are playing golf.

Frankly, I think there has been a good deal of nonsense written about concentration, and I fear the result in many cases has been to get many golfers even more tense than they were before.

I have just said that to be a successful golfer one must close the mind, to the extent that the stroke which is being played is the only thing that matters. Equally I think it is a bad thing for a business man to go on the course and all the way round worry whether he should make this decision or that decision or whether he should invest money in one undertaking or another.

You cannot solve problems like than *when you are playing a stroke*. It may be possible to think about things between strokes; many people can do this most successfully and no doubt feel quite relaxed, because they are able to shut off their mind except when they are playing the actual stroke.

But to play first-class golf it is necessary to play every stroke in the very same way, *and to do that continuous concentration should not be needed*. What you have to do is to think only of the stroke you are playing. But there is no need to get all tense. If your technique is right you should hit the ball like a machine, but without clenching your teeth and getting tied up like pieces of whipcord.

Take riding a bicycle. Once you have learned to ride a bicycle you don't have to concentrate on riding it every time you go out. You ride the bike subconsciously as long as you are on a wide quiet road. But what happens if you decide you are going to ride your bike through a very narrow opening or across a narrow plank?

At once you start to think about what will happen if you fall off the machine—you start thinking about the penalty of wobbling and misjudgement. You concentrate like mad and then it's two to one you'll fall off or run into the wall.

It is the same with golf. Have you ever thought how your shots would fare if you played on a course which had fairways 300 yards wide? I think you would hit the shots straight down the fairway with complete confidence. Why? Because you are not concentrating on putting the ball on a certain part of the fairway or trying to avoid trouble.

So you see if concentration means thinking about the trouble ahead and the possible penalties if you get in bunkers or gorse, then I do not agree that concentration will help you to play better golf. *It will do nothing of the kind*. Where concentration will help is when it co-ordinates all the movements necessary to make a good golf shot.

You have often heard the word "temperament" used in describing some golfer or another. What is temperament? To my mind it means the correct balance between body and mind, for make no mistake about it each has its role to play in this game of golf. If your mind and body are not correctly co-ordinated, you have a bad temperament; if your mind and body are correctly co-ordinated then you have a good temperament.

Modest golfers are modest golfers and will remain such because they have not yet acquired "good temperaments". In other words, they have not yet got sufficient self-control to shut out all the things which should be shut out. This will not come easily; it can only come after a great deal of practice and after a golf professional has demonstrated the mechanical side of the game and this has been absorbed by the pupil.

Many golfers are put off by the slightest noise or movement—this, by the way, is most noticeable when things have not been going right. This demonstrates quite clearly that anyone who is put off by a noise has not, at that moment at least, perfect co-ordination between mind and body. To give an example of this co-ordination I will repeat one story that has been going round the golf world for years. I think it is true. Anyway it is to the effect that the great woman player Miss Joyce Wethered, or Lady Heathcoat-Amory, as she now is, was putting on one of the greens at St. Andrews during a championship. She holed a difficult putt and later a friend asked her, "Weren't you put off by that train on the green?"

The great golfer is said to have replied: "What train?"

Clearly she was able to shut everything from her mind except the correct movements of hitting the golf ball, but I'm sure she was never tensed up.

I cannot close a chapter on the mental attitude without touching on the subject of keeping the head down. "Head up," and any tendency to look at where the ball is going to land before it has been struck, must be nipped in the bud at once. If it isn't, then I can only suggest that the most dire consequences will follow.

Do not confuse the expressions "Head Up" and "Head Still". Not so long ago many golf professionals used to tell their pupils they must keep their heads rigid. I've watched a number of golf films and I've never seen a golfer's head rigid yet while he has been swinging. When you take a full swing, the head must move slightly in its plane but only slightly.

It is true to say I've seen some golfers concentrate so hard on keeping the head still that they failed to deal successfully with the matter on hand—the swing. My advice to you is to see that the head is still but not to the extent your whole body is tensed up.

Many people try to keep their heads rigid because they have made up their minds to keep their eye on the ball. The necessity for keeping your eye on the ball is obvious. You must look at an object if you are going to hit it, but there is no reason why you should over-do things.

If you are completely confident that the methods you are employing are as near perfect as you can make them, then I believe that you will not be tempted to look up before you hit the ball. It is uncertainty and anxiety which make you want to lift your head to see where the ball is going to finish up. In other words, because you have lost confidence in your swing, you are afraid of the outcome of your stroke.

BE FAMILIAR WITH THE RULES

ONE of the first things any budding golfer must do is to study the rules of the game. A book of the rules is sure to be in your clubhouse, but I am afraid it is not made as much use of as it might be. Even among experienced golfers, and here I am not excluding professionals, there is a widespread ignorance of the rules of the game. It is deplorable but it is a fact. If you are beginning the game therefore, make sure you know what you can do on a golf course and what you cannot do.

There is a great danger that when friends are playing golf they do not play strictly to the rules. They take liberties in other words, because of laziness perhaps or because they don't want to play too seriously. This is a bad outlook and you should always play to the rules, because although no harm is done in friendly matches, what happens when you come to play in a competition? By that time not playing strictly to the rules might have become second nature to you, and believe you me if you do not play according to the rules in a competition you will soon be told about it, and rightly so. And even worse, you might quite easily make yourself liable to disqualification.

There are many rules of golf—some people think too many—and it is impossible for me to mention them all here, but I will say something about a number of them in the hope that by so doing they will become more deeply imprinted on your memory and enable you to play golf in the correct manner. In any case any players agreeing to waive rules are liable to be disqualified.

The first shot you hit in a round of golf is from a teeing ground, but you cannot tee up anywhere in the area. The ball must not be put on its peg in front of the markers and it must not be more than two club lengths behind them.

"Air shots" are not unknown among the more humble golfers. By "air shots" I mean misses. In a competition an air stroke counts as a stroke; but if the ball falls off the tee peg without being hit that does not count as a stroke, although some people seem to think it does.

Once the ball has been hit off the tee, it should not be touched again until it is taken out of the hole. There are several exceptions to this. For instance, you can lift the ball to identify it if it is impossible to see the markings on the ball, or when the ball has become so badly damaged that it is impossible to continue with it. In either case you should consult your opponent or partner first. You may also have to lift your ball from water, which you are entitled to do, or from a piece of the course which is marked "Ground Under Repair". On the putting green you may lift your ball if you think your ball is helping to give your opponent a line to the hole or when your opponent asks you to lift the ball as it is in his way. In each case on the putting green you must mark the spot from which you have lifted the ball and replace it on that spot.

It might so happen that when you are starting golf the ball will find its way into places where there are bushes, heather, trees or very long grass. Make sure before you play the ball that it is yours, for in match-play if you played a ball which did not belong to you, you would lose the hole, and in stroke-play you would have two strokes added to your score. If by some mischance you play your opponent's ball and he plays yours, you both play out the hole as if nothing untoward had happened. It is always a good thing, before you start, to show your opponent or partner the ball with which you will be playing, so that he will not choose a ball of the same make and with the same markings.

Now there is the question of a ball being lost or having been hit out of bounds. What you have to do then is to go back to where you played the stroke and play another ball, counting both strokes and adding a penalty stroke. In golf you will often hear golfers speak of "stroke and distance". It is this penalty for a lost or out of bounds ball which they are discussing.

If your ball does go into the trees or into bushes or into the rough you are not allowed to smooth down the grass, or break or bend bushes, twigs or branches in order to improve the lie of the ball and be able to hit the ball better. You are allowed to take up what is called a "fair stance", but no intentional or unintentional bending or breaking, please.

Then there are bunkers. You must not touch the sand in the bunker with your club, nor are you allowed to pick any object out of the bunkers before you play the shot.

If you are in the act of playing a shot on the fairway or in the rough, i.e. you have stood up and addressed the ball by laying your club behind it prior to making a stroke, and the ball moves, you must count an extra stroke.

There are also times when your ball may be stopped or deflected by somebody or by some object while it is still moving. You take no notice of this, but play the ball as it lies, where it comes to rest; but if your ball is lifted and carried away by a person, or perhaps a bird or animal, you get back the ball if you can and replace it as near as possible to the spot where it was lying originally.

Perhaps here I should say that if you have occasion to drop a ball, you do it in the approved manner by standing with your face to the hole and dropping the ball over your shoulder. If it is not possible to drop a ball without it rolling nearer the green you are allowed to place it, and if you drop a ball and it rolls into a bunker or out of bounds or to a point two clubheads or more from where you are standing you can drop it again free of charge. If in such cases it is not possible to keep it from rolling, then you can place it.

I think that covers a good many points on the fairway and in the rough, etc.; now I will go on to say something about the rules as they affect you when you are on the green.

When you are on the putting green you can leave the flagstick in the hole, have it held by your opponent or by a fellow competitor, or you can have it taken out of the hole altogether, but you cannot leave the flagstick and then have it removed while the ball is in motion. If a player's ball hits the flagstick while it is being held the player loses the hole in match-play or suffers a two-stroke penalty in stroke-play; but there is no penalty if the player has not asked anyone to hold the flagstick and it is therefore unattended.

On the putting green you can pick up any loose pieces of grass or leaves or anything similar and you are also allowed to clean your ball. If, when you are playing to a green, your ball lands on an adjacent one you must pick up the ball and take it off the green to a spot the same distance away from the hole to which you are playing.

As with strokes through the green, i.e. on the fairway, the player whose ball is farthest away from the hole plays first. He can ask his fellow competitor or opponent to remove and mark his ball if it is in the way. If, when you are putting, your ball strikes that of a fellow competitor, you suffer a two-stroke penalty; that is in stroke-play. In match-play, if your ball strikes that of an opponent, the opponent may replace his ball, but if it has gone nearer the hole he will obviously leave it where it is; there is no penalty involved here.

So much then for what you can do and what you cannot do; but I say again it is best for you to familiarise yourself with the rules, for I have explained only a few of them here. A pocket rule-book is available in most golf clubs, and you should make sure you get hold of one and so save yourself from much embarrassment later on. Don't forget also that committing a breach of the rules is not looked on with pleasure by other golfers, and in a competition it may well lead to your being disqualified.

GOOD MANNERS IN GOLF

GOOD manners and consideration for others. Do we all possess those attributes? Many people, or perhaps I should say most people, do in the ordinary run of things, but it is a fact that some men, and women too, I suppose, who are good-mannered and considerate to their family and to the public in general, are apt to become a little selfish when they go out on the golf course.

Why that should be so I have no idea, except perhaps that enthusiasm carries some people away to such an extent that they think only of their own game and have little regard for others. But please do not think that such people are in the majority. Not by a long way. Indeed the number of golfers who deliberately cause a nuisance to their fellow members are very few and far between.

There are the instances where things happen by accident. For instance, it is simply not done to play until the golfers in front are well out of range so that there is no danger of your ball hitting them or interfering with their game. Yet occasionally a golfer might wait until those in front are a long way off and then hit the shot of his life which flies among the people in front. In such circumstances an apology should be tendered at the first possible opportunity.

Then conversely you should not hold up the players behind you. If you have had to look for a ball, or have been in a series of trouble spots, it may be that the players following have had to wait for long periods. It is best for everyone that you wave the following golfers on, and allow them to go on and play in front of you. They will appreciate the gesture and you will enjoy your game more because you are not being hustled.

Then there is the case of a lost ball. The time allowed for looking for a ball is five minutes. After that you must play on. But often I notice at clubs where four-ball matches are the vogue that when a ball is lost all players have a little search and then three of them go on to play out the hole. It appears that some clubs approve of this idea. I am afraid I do not. Everyone should help look for the ball until the time-limit is up and then move on, allowing those following to pass through if necessary. I have no objection if the players continue the search after five minutes have gone, as long as they do not hold up the players behind. Here I should say that all golfers should walk at a brisk pace between shots, and I think that those of you who have seen me play will agree that I practise what I preach in this direction.

Never stand behind your partner or opponent as he is playing his stroke, for he may just catch a glimpse of you out of the corner of his eye, and this is most disconcerting. The proper place to stand is some distance away, directly opposite or at least almost opposite the way he or she is facing when addressing the ball.

Some golfers have been known to introduce a little gamesmanship by coughing, or moving just as their opponent is about to play a stroke. Such conduct is to be condemned, and thankfully it is rare.

On the same subject I notice that a good many beginners start to move off just before their partner or opponent has completed his stroke. This is done because they have probably hit a good shot and are anxious to get after the ball. But it can be very upsetting to the player who is in action.

Somewhere or other, either in a clubhouse or on notices on the course, you will have seen the words "Replace All Divots" or "Divots Must Be Replaced". It may be that your golf is not at the stage where you take divots in the same way as the stars do, but I am afraid there will be many times when you knock a great hole in the ground because you have played a bad stroke. That chunk of ground must be replaced and tamped down. If you do not do that, and no other golfer does it either, the course will suffer greatly.

More than that, it is certain that from time to time the ball played by other golfers will land in the holes and they will be penalised for the selfishness and stupidity of others.

Much the same applies to bunkers. When you go into a bunker and have played the ball out see that you take your club and smooth out the sand where the ball has been lying and where you have made footmarks. As you leave the bunker cover over the marks as you leave the sand. There is nothing more infuriating than seeing your ball lying in someone else's clubmark or footmark in a bunker.

I think these remarks dispose of several of the most important points "through the green", by which I mean from tee to green; and now I will say something about the things one mustn't do on the green.

First of all, never take your bag of clubs on to the green with you. Leave them lying at the side. Naturally the same applies to a trolley. Always be careful that the wheels of the trolley never at any time go on any part of the green, even the edge. The place for clubs and trolley is well off the green. The only thing you can possibly need on the green is your putter.

If you are taking the flagstick out of the hole, do it carefully so as not to damage the side of the hole. Having taken it out, place it gently on the green well away from the hole. If you throw it down the sharp end is liable to damage the green, and even if it falls flat the stick can still damage the green.

On the green you should stand well away from the player who is putting, and I need hardly say that as with shots through the green you should not move or chatter to another player.

If there are no caddies, you should ask your opponent whether or not he wants the flagstick held, or left in the hole, or removed from the hole. You should also ask him, if your ball is near his line, whether he wishes your ball to be lifted and the spot marked by the placing on the green of a coin or a special disc used for the job.

Many greens are in very close proximity to tees, although in most cases the tees are a few yards away or more. Where the tees are at the very side of the greens, it is customary to allow the golfers on the tee to play off before starting the work of getting the ball into the hole. This is a matter of common sense, for not only will you be putting off the player who is driving, you might well be struck by a wayward ball if your attention is focused on your own putting stroke.

I am afraid I have seen many golfers, especially beaten golfers, walk off the last green without having the courtesy to congratulate their opponents. In friendly matches this habit may not be so common as it is in big-time golf, but for myself I see no wrong in the loser thanking the winner for the game and then walking off the green with him. So many golfers, after they have been beaten, walk off the green almost before their opponent has holed out. I regard such an action as very bad-mannered.

Apart from manners on the course, most clubs have certain rules and regulations by which all members must abide. There is the matter of dress. In the past almost every club insisted that all members and visitors should appear in the bar and in the dining-room wearing jackets and collars and ties.

To a certain extent that regulation has been lifted in many clubs as far as going into the bar is concerned, and golfers can now enter the bar wearing a shirt or pullover and without a tie. This has come about, I think, because some of the sports shirts which are worn by many golfers are quite unsuited for ties. I am sure there must be very few golf clubs, if any, in Britain at least, which allow players to enter the dining-room without wearing a jacket and a collar and tie.

In other countries golf clubs are quite indifferent to attire, and shirt sleeves or pullovers are the thing everywhere in the club. We must not forget that in most of these countries the weather is a good deal warmer, which accounts for the laxness in this question of wearing apparel.

I am telling you all this because, when you join a golf club or visit another one, you should ascertain what the general custom is about dress. If you cannot find out anything or you are too embarrassed to ask them the thing to do is play safe.

Mention of visiting other clubs reminds me that when you do, you should go to the secretary, or the steward if the secretary is not available, and ask if it is all right to take out a ticket for a round of golf or for a day. Most golf clubs welcome visitors, though there are still a few which insist on certain qualifications such as a letter from the secretary of your own club.

On no account go to a strange club and start playing without paying a green fee. Not only is that bad manners but it also raises the matter of insurance.

Not so many years ago there was a case of a visitor going out to a club. It was a small club and there was nobody around to take his money and sign him in. During his round his ball struck a man who subsequently died. In the course of time there was a lawsuit and the unfortunate golfer, already desolate as a result of the accident, had to meet a large claim himself.

You may well say: "That was a very unusual case and is not likely to happen to me!" My answer to that is that you never know.

My advice is that when you join a club or visit a strange club, just keep in the background for a bit and take stock of what goes on around you. Members of clubs do not like new-comers coming and being presumptuous. Better to have no notice taken of you than too much, but I think that you will find that generally speaking you will be made to feel at home when you go into any club; for golf is a grand and friendly game, and the people who play it are in the main grand and friendly people.

ON PRACTISING

As far as I can see, only the most enthusiastic golfers indulge in practice. The great majority come to the golf club, change as quickly as they can and then dash on the tee, not even taking time to have a couple of practice swings, far less twenty minutes on the practice ground.

This is very wrong, but there are reasons for this kind of thing. Many golfers, indeed most golfers, can play only at week-ends and they want to use every moment they can spare to golf in going round the course, not in hitting shots on the practice ground. I must say I can't blame them for that outlook, but it is not calculated to improve their golf. I say here and now that such tactics will not only not improve the game but in time will make it go back.

Practice is essential if one's game is going to improve. *But it must be the right kind of practice.* So often do I see at various golf clubs men and women spending hours hitting a golf ball and showing no improvement at all at the end of their labours.

They are trying to hit the ball farther and straighter, but having no idea what to do in order to bring about improvement, consequently they are more or less wasting their time.

If your practice is to pay dividends, then you must know what you are trying to do. It is quite useless going out on the practice ground just to hit shots aimlessly. All that will happen is that you will become bored and as a result your game will get worse.

In this book I have told you how you can correct certain faults in playing golf. If you suffer from any of these faults then read the chapters carefully, digest what I have said and then go out on the practice ground, bearing in mind my various hints.

Here I must make it clear that the written word is only a substitute for a personal lesson from your professional. I can only write in general terms, but your professional can take stock of you personally when he sees you hit a few shots. He is able to see at a glance your age, build and capabilities, and so is in the best position of anybody to give you advice on what you are doing wrong.

The best time to go on the practice ground to correct faults is immediately after a lesson from your professional. There is no doubt at all about that. Then you are fresh and have in your mind all the things he has told you. It takes a great deal away from the value of your professional's lesson if you have the lesson, then go home. But you will be surprised at how many golfers do just that.

There may be times when you want to go on the practice ground, although you feel you have no apparent faults in your game. At such times you must remember all the various points about what you have to do. Such practice should be carried out regularly.

If you go to the big tournaments and watch the professionals practising, you will notice that every so often they turn and have a chat with their neighbours. This is to prevent them getting too tense and also to keep them from getting bored. Some golfers thrive on practice and can go on all day without getting stale. To others practice is a penance to be avoided at all costs.

I dislike too much golf theory. It merely confuses, but all the same, practice without some thought is quite useless. For instance, it is no use going out to the practice ground with your number 4 iron with which you have been slicing, if you don't know how to go about curing a slice.

We all go off one particular club at some time or another, and so it is wise to go out and try to iron out the kinks. Do not take out a variety of clubs if it is only the one that is causing you trouble. Then, if you know what you are trying to do, get busy. I believe that *knowing what you are trying to do* is the key to successful practising.

Mind you, I am not decrying the fellows who go to the practice ground to "hit a few shots" before playing a round. On the contrary, that is very valuable time spent, for the hitting of a few shots loosens up the muscles so that when they start to play their round they ought to be able to get things going from the word "go".

But even "hitting a few shots" should not be done aimlessly, for if it is, a fault can develop right away and you will spend half the round or more trying to get your game right.

While keeping in mind that the long game in golf is very important, I think that most golfers of modest handicaps should devote most of their time on the practice ground to the short game. A good short game will bring down your handicap quicker than anything, far quicker than being able to drive the ball long distances. Long hitting is very valuable but only if backed up by a tight short game.

I firmly believe that if every long-handicap golfer would go out with his No. 6, 7 or 8 iron on every available opportunity, his game would improve enormously. The crux of the whole thing is "every available opportunity". If you are not prepared to give much or any time to practice on the score that you would rather play a round, then, as I have said, you will make little or no improvement except when you play three or four or more times a week. And if you can afford to give that amount of time to playing golf you can afford time to practise.

Inexperienced golfers are not good at getting out of bunkers, yet I am sure that you see very few fellow members of your club practising getting out of bunkers. It is really quite extraordinary this shyness about practising bunker shots, but it is true. I would certainly advise you to practise shots from a trap.

Your friends will laugh at you. That goes without saying. As they stand at the nineteenth looking through the window at you, you will have to put up with a number of ribald remarks. But I shouldn't worry about that; the chances are that you will be taking the half-crowns when next you meet on the course.

Then there is putting. Almost every golf club has a practice putting green, and I advise you to spend some time on that putting green every time you go to the club. If it is permissible to use one of the greens on the course for practice so much the better because actual greens are very often truer than are putting greens.

But you must treat putting practice seriously. Don't fool about when you are on the putting green. Try to get some degree of concentration into the thing.

I find that many people, when they are on the putting green, give themselves too many putts. Every time the ball goes to within about two feet of the hole they drag the ball away with their putter on the assumption that two-foot putts are hardly worth bothering about.

How wrong! These putts are just what I call "the miserable ones", the ones which trouble you when the tension is on. In the United States, in friendly games when there are four or five players engaged, every—and I repeat *every*—putt is holed out, no matter if it is only a couple of inches away from the hole. Always remember that when you are having practice *never give yourself anything*.

I suppose practice in getting out of the rough is too much to expect. I must say I have seen very few long-handicap players doing that. I suppose most of them feel that they get too much practice in getting out of the rough when they are playing a round. The only reply I can make to that is that it can be expensive in the matter of wasted strokes.

Still, I don't want to labour this practice business too much. I do realise that many people have little time to give to rounds of golf, far less to practice; but I must make something of this subject because practice can play such an important part in making progress at golf.

If you have no time to practise, then perhaps you have a back garden, and if you have, then half an hour's swinging at a golf club will do you a vast amount of good. It will keep the muscles in trim to a certain extent and will also keep you in touch with the game. Some of my amateur friends who are unable to play much golf tell me that if they are away from it for weeks sometimes they feel less inclined to play when the opportunity occurs. There may be something in that, so some practice swinging in the back garden will keep you in the mood.

TAKING CARE OF YOUR EQUIPMENT

AFTER playing golf for some time, or even at the very start, you will have provided yourself with pretty good clubs, golf shoes, waterproofs and the like. I think I have suggested elsewhere that a novice can get along for a little without a great deal of special equipment, but sooner or later, of course, he must provide himself with the real stuff.

Some people are naturally good at looking after their belongings. You notice that with cars, many are always clean and look spick and span while others have a dirty, uncared-for look. For myself, having had to struggle in my early days to buy anything I set my heart on, I have always taken good care of everything I possess.

That policy has paid me, I think, for in the end it saves me money. In addition to that, there is always the pride of possessing something of which you can be proud.

I can tell you it will pay you to look after your golf clubs, shoes and other equipment. Let us start with the clubs. Nowadays all golf clubs are rustless so no longer have they to be cleaned like the old clubs I can remember. When I was a boy at Surbiton I used to spend many weary hours cleaning and polishing the irons of the various members.

I was heartily sick of the sight of them, and it has often struck me since that the Surbiton members must have been the most fastidious golfers in the world.

That is all finished, but still you would be wise to keep a piece of cloth handy and rub over all your clubs at the end of each round. It may not do them an enormous amount of good, but at least it will help them to retain their appearance, and that is useful if you should want to sell them at some future date! The grips should also be treated to take the grease off them and to soften them. You can buy preparations for the purpose, but many people use a mixture of methylated spirits and castor oil in equal proportions.

Perhaps the care of your golf shoes is more important than anything else as far as equipment is concerned. Many people take a long time to break-in shoes, so care has to be taken in choosing them. There are many various kinds of golf shoes, and it depends on you which kind you like. For myself, I should say that the best all-round pair is a pair which is not too heavy.

Heavy shoes are splendid in the British winter, but in the summer they can be rather heavy for some. If you are big and strong and your feet never worry you then this substantial shoe is the thing, but generally if you possess only one pair of golf shoes, and most golfers do, then a pair not too heavy may suit you better.

When you get new golf shoes, you should rub them regularly with one or other preparations which are sold for the purpose. Some people stick to the good old dubbin. Such treatment helps to keep your shoes waterproof and soft.

If you do not do that, it is likely that when you go to the club after a couple or more months' absence your shoes will be as hard as boards, and naturally most uncomfortable. In addition to keeping shoes soft, most preparations also possess qualities which help to keep them waterproof. It is important that they should be waterproof, for in winter in Britain some courses get very wet, hence the emphasis on shoes which keep out water in all circumstances.

Of course you cannot keep the water from coming over the top of your shoes if you wade into marshy ground or trample through long wet grass. Then all you can do is to go into the clubhouse and change your socks. You should always take to the club with you a spare pair in case of emergency.

While I am on the subject of changing socks, may I say that while most golf clubs have showers, etc., it is extraordinary that so few members make use of them. There is great danger from getting a cold after a wetting on the golf course, and I commend to you a hot shower after you come in damp and miserable. It will do you more good than a visit to the nineteenth.

If you do come in wet, see that you make arrangements for your pullover, slacks, etc., to be dried. Don't just crumple up your waterproof equipment and stuff it into the foot of your locker. Again, many golfers are very careless about this, though certain golf clubs are partly to blame for allowing dirty, wet clothing to be hung up and lie about the changing room. Some changing rooms are disgraceful.

Then there is your trolley. How often do you give it a little bit of a service? I know dozens of golf-club members who take their trolley out of the shed, pull it around the course and then push it back into the shed. Sometimes they don't even put it away. They just leave it lying about any old where. Admittedly there are not a great many movable parts to a golf trolley, but all the same a drop of oil and an occasional clean will enhance its appearance and increase its efficiency.

Then what about those men with old, dirty slacks and ancient, torn pullovers? Some of them might well take a thought about their appearance. I suppose when I write on that subject I am banging my head against a stone wall, so to speak, because many men who are extremely well dressed in their everyday life take a sort of pride in going about like scarecrows on a golf course. I cannot think why they do it, but they do.

Generally speaking, what is needed in the care of golf equipment is just a little common sense. If any of it gets wet, for instance, it must be dried slowly but thoroughly and must not be bundled away. Shoes must first be cleaned and then dried and treated as I have suggested earlier in the chapter, trolleys should be oiled occasionally; and apart from the equipment see that you yourself do not stand around or sit around with wet socks and damp clothing. Of course, if you invest in a really good waterproof suit more than half your troubles are over.

PART FOUR
Question and Answer

I am thinking of taking up golf. How many clubs do you think I need to start with and how much will all my equipment cost? I suppose it is also wise to join a club. How do I go about this, and what is the average subscription?

I started playing with one club. Far too many people think that to play golf you have to arm yourself with fourteen clubs like the pros. Six clubs are plenty to begin with; in fact, for quite a long time these six are all you need. Most professionals' shops these days have a stock of very good second-hand clubs, though I'm against anyone starting with old clubs as they were made for the original owner and not for you, and as the lie of the clubs invariably determines how you will swing. If that lie isn't a good one your swing may cultivate a very bad groove which later on will be very difficult to put right.

Prices of clubs are from the cost of one at £1 second-hand to £5 10s. or so. That range will offer a price to suit every pocket; in other words, equipment is as expensive as you want it to be.

Joining clubs is just like joining anything else. Get to know someone at a club and get them to propose you. At least that is the procedure in the London area where most clubs are full as far as new members go. Fees vary up and down the country. There are places where it is possible to play for a couple of pounds a year and others where the fees are up to £30 or so; these are in the big cities, and even there it is possible to join these clubs for a small fee as an artisan member. The latter entails certain restrictions at weekends, such as having to start before a certain time and not until after another time. There are also public courses where one doesn't have to be a member, and where you just go along and pay for your round.

Every time I have a golfing holiday at the seaside and the wind blows a little more strongly than usual, my whole game collapses. Why is this, and can you help me?

This golfer, who obviously plays on a course near a town, is no exception. So many inland courses are protected by trees and houses that the golfers who play on them never encounter what I should call a really strong wind. It is in this department that the people who belong to seaside courses have a real advantage. To them the wind is just another hazard and most of them learn how to use it to the best advantage. They do not worry about it and become panic-stricken. In fact, they enjoy the challenge.

One of the strongest winds I can remember having to face in competitive play was in the Open Championship of 1938 at Sandwich. During the night before the final day the wind rose to gale force, tearing branches from trees, and when we arrived on the course the next day the place was in a shambles. Tents had been blown down and the prospect of playing and trying to do a good score was certainly pretty frightening. Golf enthusiasts will remember that the day marked one of Henry Cotton's greatest rounds. He went round in 74—a remarkable effort in the conditions. I remember I took 83, not very good, I know, but my, the wind was strong.

How, then, can one combat the wind? First remember that a really well-hit shot will not be affected very much by the wind, especially if the ball is kept low.

Let us start with the driver. To keep the ball low it is obviously a help to tee the ball lower than usual. When you hit the ball make sure the stroke is a good firm one and keep the hands just a little in front of the clubhead. The stance should be a little wider than usual and the footwork kept to the minimum. The key word for playing into the wind is steadiness, and balance is all-important.

If you are playing an iron into the wind, remember to take one or two clubs more than usual and let the clubhead do the work; don't try to force the shot. Hit well down and through the ball and be careful not to sway. Then you will get that low, long, boring ball which will be the envy of all your opponents.

Now let us consider a wind that blows from right to left. Obviously the slightest suspicion of a pull when the wind is in this direction will be fatal. First, place your right hand more on top of the shaft to keep the clubface open. Aim down the right-hand side of the fairway and open the stance. At the same time hold on more tightly with the left hand. Of course the degree to which you do these things depends on the strength of the wind.

If you are a slicer then the wind that blows from left to right is a real problem. To play in this wind put your right hand more under the shaft and aim to the left of the fairway. Some people say you should close the clubhead at the same time but this is risky and best left to the experts.

Now what about a wind behind you? The great secret here is to play so that the wind will help you. If you want length off the tee, tee the ball high so that it will go quickly up into the air. Any tendency to try to hit the ball harder must be avoided.

The difficulty when the wind is behind comes when you have to judge approach shots. The run and the flight will be greater when the wind is behind and allowance has to be made for this.

Many good golfers faced with a strong wind take a shorter grip on the club, and this is a good idea for it gives you greater control. Another tip worth remembering is that the wind does not blow so strongly near the ground, and therefore the short shots are best played as run-ups.

One of the main reasons the average golfer has so much difficulty playing in the wind is because he gets into a panic. He tries to hit too hard and the whole rhythm of his swing is thrown out of gear. So when the wind is blowing, try to swing even more smoothly and slowly, and do not hit harder. Balance is essential for successful play in the wind; if you start lashing at the ball you will lose this and your whole game will collapse.

Most professionals seem to play with deep-faced wooden clubs, but when I went to buy a new set of woods from my own professional he tried to sell me a set of shallow-faced clubs. Which do you think are best for players in the 10 to 18 handicap range?

This is purely something for the choice of an individual and I would trust your professional's advice. I am sure your pro knows your game and what would suit your methods better than I do without seeing you. I know I prefer my driver to have a fair-size face—not one of those ridiculously deep instruments I have seen, however.

Do you advise keeping the hands slightly in front of the clubhead at the address position, and should they be held high or low?

Not really. If you address the ball with a slight angle to the right, clubhead, shaft hands, left arm and the hands are behind the ball for a driver. The moving of the ball back to the right as you go down the golfing armoury will tend to bring the hands in front of the ball. If you stand to the ball and feel you have to reach out to get to it (i.e. standing too far away) your hands will be too high, and vice versa if you stand too close.

One hears a great deal these days about the American method of playing golf. What is this American method and why is it considered so much better than any other?

Flat clubface at the top of backswing, arrived at by rolling open the wrists and dropping them behind the shoulders rather than above as per upright swing at the top—this is the method you mean.

It is debatable whether this method is better than any other method, but seeing that the majority of golfers tend to slice, this method does put one in a position to stop the slice.

I have great difficulty in reading the greens on courses to which I am a stranger. Can you give me some things to look out for when sizing up a putt?

I think, over and above the first look for the obvious slopes, that the last five feet should be closely studied for grain or nap in the grass. This has become necessary these days, more than before the 1939–45 war, as labour difficulties have necessitated the use of over-green mowers and the continuous cutting around and around has made the grass lie one way on one side of the green and the other way on the other side, so that a ball now as it tends to slow down is affected by the grain. In consequence extra allowance or otherwise is necessary whichever way the grain may be running across your putt; and a much firmer putt is necessary when putting against the dark green, or not so firm when you are putting in the light green which is putting with the grain.

I have a nasty tendency to sky the ball from the tee. I have tried teeing my ball lower, but this does not really work. Do you think there is something wrong with my swing, and if so what would it be?

I don't think the height of the tee controls the trajectory of the flight of the ball at all. It appears to me your arc is too steep, and I would suggest keeping the club lower along the ground in the back-swing. This will widen the arc and concentrate on the left hand leading the clubhead through the hitting area and for a period after the spot where the ball is teed up.

My friends tell me I have a good-looking swing, but my scores are anything but good. What do you think is the trouble?

A lot of people suffer from this. A good swing does look nice, but the golf ball must be hit to make it go, i.e. faster clubhead speed at impact, without fouling up your swing, and a lot of work on the short game. This is where scores are made or marred.

Many of the leading professionals say that they are "faders". What does this mean and how does one become a fader? Is it a good thing to try and develop?

A fader is a player who tends to hit the ball slightly left to right in flight. To fade a ball a slightly open stance is adopted, the club is taken very slightly outside the line of play, then in the down-swing it returns from the outside to the inside across the ball with the clubface slightly open. In other words, a very small tendency to hit the ball a glancing blow. I do not advise anyone to cultivate a fade or hook shot for that matter. The straight ball is the one to hope to get. The fade ball doesn't fly so far as a straight one, due to the slight glancing blow imparted.

I have a good deal of trouble in playing my lofted irons. I always seem to pull the ball to the left of the green. My swing is fairly short and compact. What do you think is the trouble?

It seems that little movement is required for lofted clubs—by that I mean the feet don't move about too much. But don't think you must become immobile. On the other hand, don't wave your left heel to everyone on the golf course at the top of the backswing. You say your swing is short and compact. This is where the trouble might easily be. The short swing would, particularly if you are stockily built, tend to get you hitting too soon and this fact would make you too right-handed with your hit blocking the ball to the left. Keep the clubface open longer, try lengthening the backswing and let your left hand do a bit more work.

I have the greatest difficulty using a driver off the tee. I seem to be able to hit with all the other clubs quite well, but I do not feel I will improve while most of my second shots have to be played from heavy rough. What can I do about it?

First there is really no need to use a driver off the tee; a brassie (No. 2 wood) or for that matter a spoon (No. 3 wood) will do just as well. Certainly you might lose a little length, but ten to fifteen yards would be worth the pleasure of playing from the middle of the fairway. However, I think your main trouble is a mental one. You think you will hit the ball crooked with your driver and sure enough you do so. This is something which you will have to wrestle with on your own. A spell on the practice ground would probably bring your confidence back, and if you can't do this then, as I say, use a brassie off the tee for a while.

What do you think about when you are playing a round in a major competition?

This is really a very difficult question to answer, but I know that I try hard to think about the next shot and only the next shot. I try to forget all that has gone before and to put out of mind the fact that I may be doing well or badly. Hitting a golf ball correctly is difficult enough without outside thoughts creeping in and ruining one's concentration. This is why you will see players sometimes step away from a shot before they play it. They have heard a noise or seen something out of the corner of their eye and their concentration, which is so important, has been ruined.

There seem to be a bewildering number of shafts for golf clubs. I am a fairly hard-hitting player and often wonder if my "regular" shaft is the correct one for me. I wonder if you could give any general rules for choosing shafts?

Far too many golfers think that, because the pros who play all day and every day play with stiff shafts, they should do so as well. I think that unless you are extremely strong and play a lot the "regular" shaft is the one for you. Never have them stiffer than the "Pro-Fit S".

I find great difficulty in getting any length into my shots. My friends keep telling me I hit early. What does this mean, and is it possible to do the opposite and hit late?

Hitting early means you are back into the ball with the clubhead before your body is ready for it—this is caused by snatching the backswing. This in turn doesn't allow you to complete the full turn of the pivot curtailing the backswing. By trial and error a longer swing should be tried out until you find it is too long, which would make you hit late. Then a happy medium can be arrived at.

I am having great difficulty with my putting. Do you think a change of putters would help or do you think I would be wiser to go to my professional for a lesson on putting?

Have a lesson by all means for it is quite possible you are doing something wrong which even a new putter wouldn't put right. Once a check on method has been done, then I find a new putter helps sometimes. Always have a spare putter for a change. You haven't an idea how nice it is to go back to the first one after a few weeks with another one because that is what you will do!

Although I have not played golf for very long I have made fairly fast progress and would now like to learn some of the more advanced techniques of the game; for instance, how does one slice and hook at will?

Don't be in too much of a hurry to confuse yourself with trick shots. Learn to hit all of your shots every time and to hit them straight. Of course, there might be a time when you have to hook and slice. Then you have to alter the line of arc of the club swinging outside the ball and bring the clubhead across the ball, hitting it a glancing blow with an open face for a slice and for a hook the reverse.

I am just taking up golf and am seventeen years old. Obviously I will have to have some lessons from my local professional, but how many do you think I will need before I can venture on to the course?

In the U.S.A. they advocate watching, etc., for six months before going on the course. I don't think the people of our country would do this, but I'm sure no one, providing they want to show some improvement later, should try going around the course unless they have had twenty lessons.

Golf is improved with confidence obtained by your own successes, and there isn't anything more soul-destroying than to be hacking, hacking and more hacking, which the odd lesson and out on to the course tends to guarantee. Lessons and practice-ground work are much better than all the playing around.

There seems to be a difference of opinion among leading players as to the part the hands play in golf. Do you think the hands are important, and why?

I think the hands are very important. Far too many people try to move the ball with the shoulders and body.

The hands control the golf club, any way you look at it. The grip is done by the hands, and one's arc is usually determined by the hands.

I find that I play best if I keep my two feet flat on the ground. However, I feel I would improve if I used the correct footwork. Please could you tell me what part the feet should play in the swing, and whether you think footwork is important?

Footwork is very important. Insufficient footwork in golf can have the same effect as a flat-footed boxer who is out on his feet. Even if he could hit his opponent, the feet are not allowing him to punch his weight.

Mind you, particularly if you are tall, it is dangerous to have too much foot movement as you would become willowy and lose balance. Don't become immobile.

I have been playing golf for about thirty years and have a style which my friends describe as agricultural. Do you think it would be worth my while having lessons in an effort to try and develop a better style? My handicap is nine.

I'm all for experiment. Through the years I have tried all sorts of ways to try to make improvements. However, I feel if you have been playing thirty years one way a few lessons wouldn't hurt as I'm sure your professional would find ways of helping you to better scores with your "agricultural" swing. A lot of golf performers amongst the low-handicap ranks aren't the essence of elegance. There are quite a few who are—shall I say?—a little rough as regards their golf swing.

I have heard it said that one should play the short chip shots from just off the green in the same way as one putts. Do you agree with this, and if not how do you advise playing these little shots around the green?

I agree it is by far the best way to play the short chips. There is less margin for error. Play with a variety of clubs too; don't restrict it to one club.

I have decided that if I want to improve my golf which I now play off 16, I must practise. Do you have any set routine for practising? How can one make it more enjoyable and less of a drudge?

I can understand practice being tedious. Obviously you must bring variety into your modes of practice. Don't start with the same club every time. Here is a programme for you: (1) wedge, 7 iron, 5 iron, 3 iron, 4 wood and driver. (2) 9 iron, 8 iron, 6, 4, 2, 3 wood, 2 wood. (3) Putting and a few chip shots. (4) Bunker shots only of all distances. (5) Difficult lies. (6) Woods only. (7) Irons only. (8) Right through the bag.

I have just bought a wedge and find it rather difficult to use. Is this a common fault and do you think it worth my while persevering with the club? My handicap is seventeen.

It is a common fault. Far too many people acquire a wedge and never get a lesson in playing it. It is a heavier club than any of the others in the golfing armoury and as such it must be used differently from the other pitching clubs. For instance, the golf ball must be struck more on the down-swing and you must swing slower or because it is a heavier club it will play you instead of you playing it.

Do you think it a good idea for a comparative beginner to try and model his game on some professional and if so who would you choose as a good example of style?

The two best models of what I think is swing perfection are Alfred Padgham and Sam Snead, and I'm sure a mental picture of these two would serve you in good stead as you acquire your own groove under professional tuition.

I always get into a muddle positioning the ball in relation to the feet. Are there any general rules I should follow which might help me?

Yes. Take up your stance to your intended line of play, then place a club shaft so that it runs from ball to feet. This line will point to a spot between the two feet. Starting from the (driver) No. 1 wood, this line from the ball should strike a point approximately at the inside of the left heel, then about half an inch per club towards the right foot as you go down the armoury of equipment, i.e. No. 2 wood 1 inch, No. 4 wood 2 inch, etc.

It appears that some professionals recommend watching the ball throughout the swing while others say one does not have to watch the ball as long as one keeps the head still. What are your views on this?

The latter are correct. One can hit the ball perfectly well with eyes shut. One can see the ball very well and sway away to the right in the backswing and completely miss the ball; but if you keep your head still you will never completely miss the shot but do not tense the shoulders.

I have been playing golf for about a year and find that I have a tendency to push my shots out to the right. It is not really a slice, for the ball flies straight enough. Why is this and what is the cure?

If after one year of golf you find the only fault you have is a ball that is pushed out to the right, congratulations!

But the reason for this seems to be, insufficient turn when you are taking back the club is curtailing your swing. In consequence you are back in the hitting area before your left side is clear or ready for it, so your clubface is open at impact that small amount, and push out is the only answer.

Because of the many hazards on my course, and because I am rather wild, I am continually faced with the need to play either high or low shots. Can you tell me how to play shots like this at will?

The position of the hands in the address are all-important and, of course, as you proceed through the hitting area you must make sure they are in this same position. For a high ball the hands should be behind the ball, with the right knee slightly more relaxed in the address. That will see to it that your right shoulder is also lower. For the low ball hands should be in front, with the ball taken farther to the right in relation to the position of the feet. The tendency is to hook the ball because of the early contact with it, but if you make certain the left hand is very strong in the through swing this should straighten things out.

Having just taken up golf again after a lapse of ten years I find I have not quite got the touch I used to have. Do you think a new set of clubs would help me?

Being a business man I would never stop a person from the purchase of a new set of clubs. There are a number of things one must realise. (1) Are you as strong in the hands as you were ten years ago when you gave the game up? (2) Even if you are, the shafts in your golf clubs would have deteriorated as they must be ten to fifteen years old. I know I play a lot and hit the ball hard, but even if I don't have a new set of clubs each year I change the shafts. Have your own professional check you over and he will advise on your clubs. You will find he won't rush you into a sale, as he will have to see you if the result of his advice goes wrong.

My son is seven years old and very keen to learn to play golf. At what age do you think he should start having lessons?

Right away a couple of lessons would be the thing. Then even if he goes away from golf and doesn't play or try to play again until he is much older, the swing he was taught while young will never be forgotten. In other words, he will soon fall into the groove he was taught.

What is the most important thing to remember when starting the backswing? Is it the pivot or taking the clubhead back in a straight line?

Keep the head still. Concentrate on starting the clubhead, hands, hips and shoulders on a rotating point around the fixed axis through the head, down the spine and so to the ground as though a stake has been driven down the aforementioned parts.

Would you say that other games like tennis and squash are harmful to one's golf?

To a certain extent yes, as one tends to use so much of the right hand with tennis and squash with the idea of making the ball dip with top spin on it. On the other hand, one has to hit the ball with the right for golf. If you realise this and exercise the left hand to withstand the strong right, all is well.

My job keeps me away from the golf course for long spells at a time. I wonder if you could give some hints on how to keep my swing in trim without actually playing golf.

By having a practice swing whenever possible, preferably with a heavy club. Your professional will make you a short club heavily weighted for this purpose. Practise chipping into a chair, and putting into a tumbler; it all helps.

Why do so many first-class players use the reverse overlap grip on the putting green? What are its advantages?

The reverse overlap helps to make certain the left hand is in command and will make sure the back of the left hand is pointing towards the hole. Then, pendulum wise, the putter head should swing absolutely square to the line of the putt.

I have recently started using a left-hand glove, but some of my friends who do not wear them say it is a sign of weakness to have to play with one. They add that I would do better if I set about strengthening my left hand with exercises. What are your views?

I find when one gets a little older powers of concentration are not as easy as they were, and I'm sure, without having to tell you to grip the club firmly in your left hand, that this is done automatically for you by the layer of glove you have between shaft and hand. When one gets older one's hands tend to forget what they should do, and we all tend to relax the gripping of the club in the left hand. So I consider a left-hand glove a big help. People who have hands that perspire will of course derive a big benefit too.

People say I am playing better the last two years. I'm sure any improvement can only be due to the glove, as that is the only alteration in anything appertaining to my game.

Do you think the large or small-sized ball is best for the average amateur of, say, 10 handicap?

Golf is largely a question of your mental approach to the game. Therefore to see the small white ball looking bigger must help one's confidence in one's ability to hit it.

Mind you, if you hook or slice, the 1·68-inch ball will hook or slice quicker; and of course against any elements it stands to reason the slightly larger ball takes more effort to drive through space than its smaller brother.

How is it that professionals get such a lot of stop on their shots to the green? Indeed, sometimes the ball actually bounces backwards. How is this done?

Most average, or indeed most, golfers who do not know the right technique have difficulty in applying back spin on the ball. The reason: they have the ball too far forward in relation to the feet, i.e. the ball too near the left foot which will tend to have the driver effect on the ball hitting on the up-swing, which of course gives top spin on the ball. Bring the ball back a bit, trust the loft of the club, strike the ball on the down-swing always taking the turf after the ball.

I wonder if you could tell me how important the position of the right elbow is at the top of the backswing?

This is a controversial subject. In the old days it was said that at the top of the backswing you should be able to support a handkerchief under the right elbow. This, I think, tends to make for a narrow arch and short backswing. The two best golf swings I have seen, Padgham and Snead, allowed the right elbow a lot of movement. As long as the right elbow is close to the side early in the down-swing, that is the all-important factor.

Although I play off scratch I am not particularly long, and I feel that if I could get another ten yards or so on all my long shots I might be able to do well in high-class golf. What do you think is the best way of getting more length?

The only way to get extra length is to get faster clubhead speed at impact. Without seeing you, I wouldn't know if your swing is long enough, or whether the wrists and hands are strong enough; but these are the main points to check on if one is after the extra yards.

Can you tell me why golfers are encouraged to use the forward press and what the term really means?

The forward press means precisely what it says. Just before the backswing is started a slight forward movement towards the line of play. People are liable to overdo this, if you say it is a good thing. I say it is, as one thing one must avoid is rigidity or becoming static to the extent of becoming frozen, and this slight movement does help to start the backswing on the recoil.

Unfortunately our course is played over a great deal and the fairways are covered with divot marks. This results in many bad lies. Are there any special techniques which can be used for playing from bad lies?

Most people go about playing from bad lies with a method which defeats them before they start. When in a bad lie never try to lift or scoop the ball out of the divot mark. Take a club one more lofted than you need for the distance from a fair lie, and make sure you hit the back of the ball (not the turf behind it). Any turf you take should be after the shot where the ball is sitting. Never try the impossible. The ball should be struck with a little faster hand action through the hitting area.

I suffer from fluffing. In other words, I keep hitting the ground just before the ball. Why is this, and can you suggest a cure?

Your mental approach to this shot must be wrong. By and large, fluffing is caused by eye off the ball and a jerky jab at it when trying to hit it.

Start at the edge of the green with your 5 or 7 iron in your hand. Think you have your putter and play an approach putt with the 5 or 7. Move back 5, 10, 15 yards and extend the length of the pendulum. You should get stroke and rhythm back very quickly.

I have great difficulty in playing those little shots near the green where one has to get some loft on the ball to get it over a bunker. I always seem to hit it on the bottom of the club. Can you help?

Rather like the answer to the fluffing question. The same practice method, but not a No. 5 or 7—an 8, 9 or 10 or the most lofted pitching club you have. You must be lifting your shoulders by straightening the knees as you come through to top the ball, or hit it with the club bottom. So keep the knees relaxed throughout, to a point of exaggeration play the shot slowly, and above all let the loft of the club do the work. It is dangerous to lay the clubface open and cut across the ball unless you are very proficient.

GLOSSARY OF GOLF TERMS
ANCIENT AND MODERN

Addressing the Ball Originally "putting oneself in a position to strike the ball". Now "taking stance and, except in a hazard, grounding the club. . . ." NOT, as Sid Field maintained, to say "Dear Ball. . . ."

Albatross A score for the hole which is three under bogey (or, in America, par).

Baff To strike the ground with the sole of the club in playing the ball, and so send the ball into the air.

Baffy A wooden club used for baffing and playing lofted shots. Nearest equivalent today is the No. 4 wood.

Birdie A score for the hole which is one under bogey (or, in America, par).

Bisque A handicap stroke which the receiver can take at any stage of the match.

Blaster Heavy niblick with a broad sole introduced between the wars and used for short pitches from heavy rough, for general recovery work, and sometimes for bunker shots.

Bogey This is generally regarded as the score for each hole which should be taken by a scratch player in normal form making due allowances for average playing conditions. It is not the same as par, and, indeed, the Americans reserve the term "bogey" for a score of one worse than par. In Britain the bogey score for the course is usually two or three strokes higher than the standard scratch, or par. The term was first heard in 1891 when a competition was held at Great Yarmouth against the "ground score" of the course, as invented by a Coventry golfer, Hugh Rotherham. It is generally accepted that the name bogey was derived from the popular song of the time: "Hush, here comes the Bogey Man." In a bogey competition the golfer plays against the bogey of each hole, taking handicap strokes as in a match, with three-quarters of the difference between his handicap and "bogey's" scratch.

Brassie Now known as the No. 2 wood, it derived its name from the fact that, unlike the "play-club" or driver, it had a brass plate on the sole to save wear in "sclaffing" and "baffing" (q.v.).

Break-club An obstacle or impediment lying near the ball which might break the club. Rules now preserve golfers from most of these troubles, and clubs do not so easily break.

Bulger A wooden club having a pronounced convexity of the face.

Bunker See Hazard.

Bye The holes remaining to be played when the main match has ended.

Caddie A person who carries the golfer's clubs—in these days for thirty bob a day. Derived from the term for Edinburgh porters and another Scottish noun "cad" or "cady", meaning a carrier. No connection with tea-caddy, although golf caddies serve on the tee (q.v.).

Caddie Cart See Trolley.

Casual Water Any temporary accumulation of water visible before or after a player has taken his stance. A player may have relief without penalty from casual water.

Chip A delicate lofted stroke played from just off the putting green.

Cleek An iron-headed club which old-time golfers used for driving, for long iron shots, and often for putting.

Cock The bend of the wrists on the backswing.

Cut See Slice.

Dead A ball is said to be "dead" when it lies so close to the hole that the next putt is a "dead" certainty. (N.B.—Harry Vardon once missed the ball altogether at six inches!) A ball falls "dead" when it does not run much, if at all, after pitching.

Divot A piece of turf cut from under the ball in playing an iron shot.

Dormy, or Dormie A side is dormy when it is as many holes up as there remain holes to play. I add "in the round", because in knock-out matches it might be necessary to play extra holes. Said to be derived from the French *dormir*—to sleep. On the other hand, it might be the victim saying "Dear me".

Draw, to To impart anti-clockwise spin to the ball, thus making it veer to the left.

Dyke In Ireland, a hole in bogey.

Eagle A score for the hole two strokes better than bogey (or, in America, par).

Eclectic A score for the round achieved by taking two or more cards and counting the best score done at each hole.

Fairgreen The old name for fairway.

Fairway By custom the mown portion of the ground at each hole, excluding putting green and teeing-ground.

Featherie, or Feathery The earliest known golf ball in Britain, made from segments of hide stitched together and then stuffed hard and solid with boiled feathers.

Flagstick A movable indicator, usually with bunting attached, placed in the hole to show its position.

Flat Descriptive of the head of a club lying at a more obtuse angle with the shaft than a club with an upright lie.

Fog Moss, rank grass, etc. Not to be confused with Scotch mist.

Foozle A bad, bungling stroke.

Fore A warning cry to players ahead—probably shortened from "Look out, afore!"

Forecaddie An extra caddie employed to go forward of the match either to signal a clear course or watch the flight of the ball. Forecaddies may now only be appointed by the committee in charge of the competition.

Fourball A match or competition in which the lower score of two partners is the side's score for the hole. Alternately a party of four players scoring separately or in different partnerships.

Foursome In Britain, a match or competition team consisting of two players playing one ball by alternate strokes.

In the United States, a fourball match. The traditional foursome is alluded to by Americans as the "Scotch foursome" or "a two-ball foursome", but beware how you use that term north of the Border.

Gobble A long fast putt holed against probability.

Grassed Description of a wooden club with lofted face.

Green Traditionally the whole course, and one still sometimes reads of a championship being played "on the Green of the —— Golf Club". Also referring to the putting green (see Through the Green).

Greensome A modified form of foursome in which both partners drive and then select one of the two balls with which to complete the play of the hole.

Guttie, or Gutty In its original form (about 1848) this was a smooth sphere of solid gutta-percha, heated and shaped in a mould. It flew badly until well dented and nicked by the use of the iron club in shots, and later productions were hand-hammered to produce this effect from the start. Still later moulds were made with set patterns, and the "guttie" in its various forms (and sizes) was the sole missile for golfers until the advent of the rubber-core ball about 1901.

Half One A handicap of one stroke deducted at every second hole (relic from the days when strokes were not taken at specified holes "marked on the card").

Hanging Lie A lie which compels the player to stand higher or lower than the spot where the ball lies.

Hazard Originally this term covered the whole course except the "fair-green" and the putting green of the hole being played. Until a few years ago roads, pathways, scrapes and even whins and bushes were hazards. But now hazards are specifically defined as "any bunker or water hazard". A bunker is an area of bare ground, often a depression, which is usually covered by sand. A water hazard is any sea, lake, pond, river, ditch, surface drainage ditch or other open water-course (regardless of whether it contains water or not). A lateral water hazard is one which runs approximately parallel to the line of play and is so defined by the committee.

Head As "Badminton" points out, the head is the lowest part of the club and, to add to the anomalous description, is equipped with a face, a neck, a toe, a sole and a heel.

Also a portion of the human anatomy which, unlike the golf club-head, should remain still throughout the swing.

Hole Materially, the orifice cut by the greenkeeper in or near to the centre of the putting green, into which the ball is played. It is $4\frac{1}{4}$ inches in diameter and at least 4 inches deep. Abstractedly, one of the 18 holes on a regular course, comprising teeing-ground, fairway, rough, bunkers and putting green.

Holes Up A method of scoring in matches, now little used, by which the complete round is played and the winner is credited with the number of holes by which he is ahead at the finish.

Hook An exaggerated degree of draw (q.v.).

Hose The iron shank of iron clubheads into which the shaft fits.

Jerk A shot played so that the clubhead strikes the ball a downward blow and stops on impact.

Jigger A maid-of-all-work club with a thin, shallow, lofted blade which could be used for run-up shots, pitch-and-run shots, long steals (q.v.) and even full shots from fairway or rough.

Like as we Lie, The A term used to illustrate the fact that with the balls in their present position each side has played the like number of strokes.

Like, Playing the To play a stroke which makes your score the same as that of the opponent.

Links Generic name for the ground over which golf is played, but scarcely applicable to suburban meadow-land and more properly applying to open downs, heath or coastal areas. Originally descriptive of dunes linked by sandy hollows along the seashore on which all the great links of antiquity were situated. It is considered by many golfers that the term can be applied only to sandy seashore courses.

Loft The degree to which the face of the clubhead is set back from the perpendicular. It varies from the straight face of many putters to the extreme loft of a blaster or wedge.

Mashie A short-faced, lofted club, introduced about 1895 and popularised by J. H. Taylor, who used it to win the first three of his five Open Championships. He believed the name derived from the "masher", a young man-about-town of those days, a dude among his fellows as the mashie was a dude among clubs. The modern counter-part of the mashie is generally considered to be the No. 5 iron.

Mashie-Niblick A more modern club, equivalent to the present No. 7 iron, which had more loft than a mashie and not so much loft as a niblick (No. 8).

Medal Materially the prize awarded to the winner of a championship or big tournament as evidence of his prowess. Abstractedly a stroke competition. In the early days of golf all competitions were by matches or some combination of matches, usually for side-stakes. But with the advent of individual competitions it became necessary to devise a means of producing one winner from the field, and stroke competitions rapidly became popular. To this day many clubs hold "monthly medal" competitions as distinct from "monthly bogey" competitions, and the term "medal play" has become synonymous with "stroke play".

Nap The texture given to the surface of a putting green by the tendency of grass to grow in one direction or the other. This is rarely noticeable on British courses, but abroad and particularly where Bermuda grass is grown, the nap is so pronounced as to be a handicap for a golfer unaware of or unfamiliar with its peculiarities.

Niblick See Mashie-Niblick.

Odd, Playing the The act of playing a shot which will make your score for the hole one stroke more than that of your opponent.

Odds A term used in olden days to indicate the handicap under which a match is being played. Odds of a third meant an allowance of six strokes per round, odds of a half meant an allowance of nine strokes. It is now customary in singles matches for the weaker player to receive from the stronger three-quarters of the difference between their handicaps. In foursomes the "odds" are three-eighths of the difference.

One off Two To play a stroke which reduces the gap between the scores at a hole to one stroke. Or to win one hole from an opponent who has been leading by two holes.

Par Sometimes identified with the Standard Scratch Score, and based on various statistics, including length of run on the ball after pitching, lengths of the holes, difficulty of terrain, and the arbitrary inclusion of 35 putts (see Bogey).

Play-club An old type of wooden club with a long supple shaft designed to get the maximum amount of distance with a good-lying ball.

Plus Fours A type of Norfolk breeches cut rather more fully and with sufficient length to allow the cloth at the knee to fall completely over the knee-strap. Believed to derive not from the association with "plus four" as a champion's handicap, but from instructions given to tailors in the Guards that the trousers encased in puttees must fall "plus four" inches below the knee.

Plus Twos Current fashionable version of plus fours with a narrower cut and less fall over the knees.

Press To hit harder than one can and so risk spoiling the shot by bad timing.

Pull To send the ball in a straight line towards the left side of the course, by swinging outside-to-in with a shut face.

Push Out To send the ball in a straight line to the right-hand side of the course by playing "inside-to-out" with an open face.

Putt A stroke played on the close-mown turf which sends the ball rolling towards the hole.

Roller A player who rotates his wrists clockwise on the up-swing and anti-clockwise on the follow-through.

Rub of the Green Any interference by an outside agency with a ball in flight, after which the ball must be played where it lies.

Rubber-core ball The universal ball for golf, constructed by winding rubber tape and thread at tension round a solid or liquid core and encasing in a cover made from gutta-percha or composition. First introduced by a Dr. Haskell in America at the turn of the century, and used by Sandy Herd in winning the 1902 Open Championship (see Guttie and Featherie).

Sand-iron A club used for extricating the ball from bunkers and sandy lies. Represented in the modern set by the sand-wedge.

Scare In old clubmaking terms the narrow tapering part of the clubhead by which it was attached to the shaft.

Sclaff, or Scruff To scrape the turf with the sole of a wooden club in playing the stroke.

Secsome Modern term for a form of greensome in which the partners, after driving, each play the other's ball, after which the play of the hole is completed with one of the two.

Slice To impart clockwise spin to the ball, so sending it in a curve to the right of the fairway.

Spoon A wooden club with a fair degree of loft, used for getting the ball away from a close lie or limiting the distance of flight to less than that achieved by the brassie. In the old days there were long spoons and short spoons, represented today by the No. 3 wood and the No. 4 wood respectively.

Square A player who does not rotate the wrists in playing the stroke.

Stableford A form of bogey competition, invented by Dr. Frank Stableford, in which points are scored for the number of strokes at each hole, on the basis of one point for a score one worse than bogey, two points for equalling bogey, three points for a birdie, and so on.

Standard Scratch Score See Par.

Steal To hole an unlikely putt from a distance by a stroke which sends the ball only to the holeside.

Stroke A forward motion of the club made with the intention of striking at and moving the ball.

Stymie A situation—from which the rules now give relief—in which a ball lies in the way of another about to be putted. Believed to be derived from the Dutch *stij me*—it stops me.

Tee An eminence, once constructed from a pinch of sand, on which the ball is placed for the first stroke at a hole.

Teeing-ground A rectangular space of two club-lengths to the rear of an imaginary line between the tee-markers, within which the first stroke at a hole must be made.

Tee-markers Boxes, pyramids, plates or other prominent objects used to define the forward limits of the teeing-ground.

Tee-pegs Wooden, plastic or rubber pegs on which the ball is placed for the drive.

Texas Wedge American term for a putter when used for playing a stroke from outside the putting surface.

Third See Odds.

Three-ball Match In which each of three golfers plays his own ball.

Threesome A match in which one player plays against two golfers playing alternate shots with one ball.

Through the Green A term for a stroke which carries the ball over the putting green or, alternatively, all that part of the hole being played except teeing-ground, putting green and any hazards.

Trap See Hazard.

Trolley A wheeled contrivance for carrying the player's clubs.

Two More, The A stroke which makes one's score for the hole two strokes more than that of the other side.

Upright See Flat.

Waggle A movement of the clubhead over the ball preparatory to making a stroke.

Wedge A heavy niblick with a flanged sole which can be used either for a high approach shot or a low stopping shot with plenty of back spin.

Whins Furze or gorse.

Winter Rules Local rules, not recognised by the Rules of Golf, instituted to preserve the turf under winter conditions, and permitting the player to move the ball to a better lie by rolling it with the clubhead. Americans refer to these as "Preferred Lies".

Wrist Shot A half-shot or less played with a pronounced roll of the wrists.